"When you play in the NFL, you're part of a bigger family. That's what Jim Kelly and his children are: family! I'm thankful to have had the opportunity to see firsthand the relationship that Jim and Erin have. This book is about that and so much more. Reading this will encourage you and hopefully as a result will strengthen the relationships you have with the people you love most."

—DAN MARINO, NFL Hall of Fame,
Special Advisor to CEO and President of Miami Dolphins

"I have known the Kelly Family for many years and have witnessed what it looks like to be "Kelly Tough" on and off the football field. However, what I have learned through watching Jim and his daughter Erin during Jim's cancer fight far eclipses the best of the best. This book is an account of what it takes to live with courage in the midst of some of life's most difficult circumstances. Well done, Erin! Your NFL family is proud of you."

—BILL POLIAN, 2015 NFL Hall of Fame Enshrinee
and ESPN NFL Analyst

"The expression Kelly Tough has become like a brand unto itself. And no one epitomizes that more than 19-year-old Erin Kelly, the firstborn child of Jim and Jill Kelly. Beautiful like her mother and feisty like her father, Erin writes eloquently and intimately about faith, family and football, a cliché expression for so many but one that she embraces with all the gusto of a Jim Kelly fist pump. I've always believed that if you want to truly learn about people look at how their kids turn out. Erin Kelly is a Hall of Fame daughter and sister and her stories and insights will touch and inspire you."

—ANDREA KREMER, multi-award-winning journalist

"Kelly Tough is a beautiful, true, imperfect love story. It's a study in toughness made of more than sheer grit, but the inner kind that turns regular people into warriors. With raw honesty, the Kellys have taken their trademark family strength and turned it into a paperback jewel of hard-earned wisdom for the reader. I've cheered and cried and learned with every page. This book will move people. It has moved me."

—LISA WHITTLE, speaker, author of {w}hole and I Want God

"We have watched Erin Kelly grow from a beautiful, caring, young girl to a soldier. This young woman became a soldier while wearing her "Kelly Tough" armor. She fought bravely when her father was weak and in great pain while battling cancer. Wouldn't we all be so blessed to have a daughter who would abandon the frivolity and innocence of youth to crawl through the trenches, to go all-in and battle for us? Erin did this while simultaneously keeping the faith—not only keeping it, but growing in it. How beautiful is that? Kelly Tough is a read for everyone, everywhere, and at anytime. You will turn over the last page of this book feeling deeply inspired and armed to battle for the people you love most."

—NFL Hall of Famer THURMAN THOMAS and PATTI THOMAS

"Becoming friends with the Kelly family over the last few years has been a true inspiration, not only to the two of us, but to the entire faculty, staff, and student body of Liberty University. We are proud that Erin Kelly, the older daughter of Jim and Jill Kelly, chose to attend this university. We have watched her mature into an articulate young lady who has demonstrated to so many others how to courageously face life's trials and tribulations with faith, dignity, and optimism. Jim and Jill exhibit these same traits and I believe their story—as told by Erin—will give you strength for your own life's journey, no matter how difficult your circumstances might be."

—JERRY FALWELL (president of Liberty University)
and MRS. BECKI FALWELL

"From that first week as friends at a high school football camp...all the way through being teammates for nine years with the Buffalo Bills... and from a continuing close friendship after our football days... Every step of the way I can tell you that two things come to mind when I think about Jim: family and toughness. At every stage of his life this is his story, his mark in life. That's why it is no surprise that "Kelly Tough" is the perfect family slogan/motto/vision for the entire Kelly family. This book, written by Jim's firstborn daughter, Erin, is an inspiring family legacy that gives flesh and blood to what Kelly Tough is all about. Through reading this book, you will be blessed by the faithfulness of God and encouraged to see His hand at work in your life."

—FRANK REICH, offensive coordinator, San Diego Chargers
and former NFL quarterback

"Kelly Tough" became a household phrase in the last year as many in America watched and supported Jim Kelly during his second battle with cancer. Now in the book, Kelly Tough, readers will be encouraged to find that this kind of toughness isn't just a Kelly thing, but a way of life for all of us. We've known Jim for years. He's tough, determined, and stout-hearted. But to know his daughter and read about her courage in action as she stepped up to care for her dad, that's something admirable that we might all aspire to emulate. Yet, as you'll discover when you read this book, it's not about the Kellys at all but about finding strength and courage in the midst of life's trials. Well done!"

—MIKE GREENBERG and MIKE GOLIC
from Mike & Mike on ESPN

Hannah —
God is good !
PRESS ON !

KELLY
TOUGH

Live Courageously by Faith

Erin Kelly

EX. 14:14

ERIN KELLY with JILL KELLY

Jim Kelly

Jer. 20:9

Kelly Tough
Live Courageously by Faith

Copyright © 2015 Erin Kelly and Jill Kelly

Published by BroadStreet Publishing Group, LLC
Racine, Wisconsin, USA
www.broadstreetpublishing.com

ISBN: 978-1-4245-5018-0 (print)
ISBN: 978-1-4245-5019-7 (e-book)

Authors are represented by The Burson Agency, Nashville, Tennessee.

Unless noted, all Scripture is from THE HOLY BIBLE, NEW INTERNATIONAL VERSION®, NIV® Copyright © 1973, 1978, 1984, 2011 by Biblica, Inc.® Used by permission. All rights reserved worldwide. Scripture quotations marked (NLT) are taken from the Holy Bible, New Living Translation, copyright © 1996, 2004, 2007 by Tyndale House Foundation. Used by permission of Tyndale House Publishers, Inc., Carol Stream, Illinois 60188. All rights reserved.

Cover design by Chris Garborg at www.garborgdesign.com.
Typesetting and interior by Katherine Lloyd at www.TheDESKonline.com.

Stock or custom editions of BroadStreet Publishing titles may be purchased in bulk for educational, business, ministry, fundraising, or sales promotional use. For information, please e-mail info@broadstreetpublishing.com.

Printed in the United States of America.

15 16 17 18 19 20   5 4 3 2 1

Dedication

This book is dedicated to the two toughest people I know. To the boy who never spoke a word but demonstrated strength beyond comprehension: Hunter Boy. You will forever be my hero. I miss you more than words can say. To my daddy: I love you so much and want you to know that your struggle was not wasted. As I watched you in the midst of your battle, I witnessed strength displayed in and through your life like never before—God's strength. I will never forget what it means to be Kelly Tough!

CONTENTS

FOREWORD

Erin Kelly and her mom, Jill, certainly picked a strange person to write the foreword for an inspirational book out of the head of an inspirational young person. I have spent all of ninety minutes in Erin's company. Usually, there is some great and close professional or personal relationship that leads to someone writing the foreword for a book. But when the Kelly family reached out to ask me to do this, it took me two seconds to think about it and blurt out, "Of course I'll do it!"

I'm a pretty big believer in first impressions. In my twenty-five years at *Sports Illustrated,* I've been in the presence of a lot of famous and not-so-famous people in the sports world, and I can tell a lot about most of them from the first couple of minutes we're together. I remember in 1995 when I met Brett Favre, who, at the time, wasn't BRETT FAVRE yet, and I introduced myself and told him I'd be in town for a week to do a story on a week in the life of the Green Bay Packers. Without a second's hesitation, he said, "I guess Drew Bledsoe's not making any news this week." (Apparently Favre felt ignored by the East Coast press at the time.) Then he said whatever time I needed, whenever I needed it, just let him know, and he'd be there for me. First impressions were exactly right. He was blunt and honest, and there for me all week. We had three or four long conversations at his home and a couple of long days in quarterback meetings at the facility.

Anyway, back to Erin. I met her when her dad, Jim Kelly, the famous quarterback, was lying in Lenox Hill Hospital in New York City, prepping to start what would be a brutal round of chemotherapy and radiation for cancer of the jaw and face. She was in the room with us, quiet mostly, as Jim talked about the difficult trial he faced over the coming months.

At one point, lying there in the bed, weary, he turned his head to Erin and said: "When you're going through pain, you're what?"

No hesitation.

"Kelly Tough," she said.

When Jim spoke, no one in the family wanted pity. There were no tears—even though everyone in that family knew how the leader of the family was on the precipice of survival. There was only the dogged determination that the old man had.

But there was something else in the room that Sunday, something—is this actually a smart word to use?—*cuddly* about the family. Erin personified it. When I finished speaking with Jim, I went to another room on the floor with Erin and her mom and asked her about an Instagram picture she'd posted a week earlier, of her and her dad together in his hospital bed, watching the Syracuse NCAA basketball tournament game. Jim, as weak as a pup. Erin, strong for her dad, and devoted.

"We're a sports family," Erin said, shrugging. "I just wanted to hang out with him. I liked the photo, because it shows the realness of our family. It's the raw truth of what he's going through."

Isn't that what we all want from the people we love—the ability for them to see us as we are, and to love us just as much in the best and brightest of times and in the lowest and most troubled of times? Erin watched thousands give her dad a standing ovation when he was enshrined in the Pro Football Hall of Fame, and she's seen over the years how he's been treated as a deity in western New York because of his career as a Buffalo Bill. And now, in the tough times, there she is, taking time off from her new life, as a Liberty University student a day's drive away, to cuddle with the old man.

"He's my buddy," she said, matter-of-factly.

That's a long way around to my point: My first impression of Erin Kelly is a very good one. She is mature beyond her years. She has gotten great training on spirituality and the real world from her parents. She has a very strong core belief that she's not in control of this ship, and her father isn't either—God is. And whatever you feel about religion or your beliefs, there is something so redeeming about a person who is driven by a great conscience and a spirit of giving. All of that was present in my first impression of Erin Kelly. When I left the hospital that day, I remember thinking, *This world needs more Erin Kellys. Thousands of them.*

One other thing about Erin. She has a conviction about her dad that I hope all children can have about their parents. There is a dogged faith in God, and her father, that is both sweet and empowering as she faces her dad's illness the same way Jim Kelly faced Lawrence Taylor.

Her last words to me that day in the New York hospital: "He will fight this till his last breath. He's a Kelly."

She is too.

Peter King
Sports Illustrated and ESPN sportswriter and author

LETTER FROM JIM KELLY

Dear Erin,

Sometimes it's hard for a strong man to be gentle or a tough guy to be tender. But me, I kind of don't know how to be anything other than tough. I suppose I may have lived the expression "tough love" before it became a cliché.

As a young boy growing up in East Brady, Pennsylvania, your grandparents (my mom and dad) and my five brothers made toughness a way of life. It wasn't even like I had a choice in the matter; it was as natural as rolling out of bed in the morning. Pops was a boxer in the Navy, and although he's fairly small in stature, he boasted a strength that kept me in check when rebellion called my name. In fact, there were times he made the blitzing linebackers I faced in my pro football career look like the tooth fairy! And he made it very clear that his sons were Kelly boys, and that our Irish last name carried with it a reputation that meant something.

Although Dad was the heavy hand in the house, my mother was actually the iron lynchpin that held it all together. It's hard to believe she's been gone now for almost nineteen years. I miss her every day and wish you could have known her. And even though I didn't realize it at the time, I would have to say that Kelly toughness was most vividly exemplified through my mother. She was tough! To put up with the shenanigans of six rambunctious boys with skyrocketing testosterone levels, she had to be. Oddly, it was in the midst of Mom's weakness and frailty that I began to really learn what true strength is all about. Mom suffered from emphysema for years and lived on oxygen and breathing treatments until her last breath. Even in the midst of suffering she rarely complained. And though it may defy stereotype, that's truly when I learned to understand what it means to be Kelly Tough—through watching my aged mother's strength in her weakness.

Then my only son, your little brother, Hunter, was born and everything changed. He was the protégé who would follow in his father's footsteps. He was supposed to beat all the records and pile up more stats and accolades than his daddy ever achieved. He was destined for greatness beyond anything I could've ever hoped for or imagined for him. Hunter was going to be the hero. He was and he still is, as you know, but in a way that none of us ever expected.

After being diagnosed with the fatal genetic disease at four months of age that we thought would take him by age two, what a battle his life became. We watched Hunter suffer every single day of his eight and a half amazing years of life. We all watched so helplessly as he fought every hour of every day. And yet, with each and every battle, our Hunter Boy displayed courage like I've never witnessed before. Through the strength I saw in Hunter's weakness, again I learned what it looks like to be Kelly Tough. I witnessed firsthand what it means to walk by faith and not by sight through watching your mom care for our son. Yes, Hunter achieved more in his short life than I will ever achieve in the days the Good Lord gives me here on this earth.

When I see the bumper stickers around town and hash tags on social media; when I hear fans shout, "Kelly Tough," amid the roar at Ralph Wilson Stadium, I'm ever mindful that although toughness is my trademark, I've come to learn through suffering that weakness and humility are of greater worth in God's sight. It is in my weakness that God is strong, not my strength or ability to take a hit and still score. Because of *His* power and victory, through

Him, in my weakness I am more than a conqueror—over defeat, cancer, and death.

I'm deeply humbled by what you have written in this book. You are an amazing young woman of God destined to do great things in this generation for God's glory. But you still have a lot to learn and more living to do. As your father, I hope and pray that you will remember what God has done in the midst of our family's greatest heartbreaks. I hope that the true meaning of what it is to be "Kelly Tough" will be displayed in your life so that all will see and know that God can and will do immeasurably more than all we could ever ask or imagine.

And although you may be a girl, I hope that when you have children someday you'll teach them the Kelly football grip and how to post up and school the boys on the basketball court— like I taught you. But, more importantly, I hope that when you go through the valley, with its sense of despair and defeat, you'll remember all that God has carried you through thus far and that He will continue to uphold you and be your strength. Oh, and lastly…Erin Marie, you're a Kelly; don't ever forget what that means.

I love you,
Daddy

INTRODUCTION

'd rather this book never existed. Or maybe I should restate that and say cancer wasn't supposed to be part of my story. Our family experienced the heart-shattering loss of my younger brother, Hunter, in 2005. When you go through something like that, you kind of assume you've been through the worst and that the other shoe dropped when the first one did. But that's not the case with our family. No, we've not ventured into the kind of valley of death that Job did (thank God), but we've had a tough go of it over the last decade or so. And it's been hard—really hard.

As the older daughter of an NFL Hall of Famer and legend, I'm going to share some of the darkest moments and brightest miracles of my life with you as I watched my father, who won countless battles on the gridiron, battle an enemy bigger and stronger than any he met on the field—cancer.

But that's not really what this story is about.

Oh, and don't let the title fool you, this isn't by any stretch of the imagination a "be all you can be, no pain, no gain" type story. Toughness is overrated. Trust me—I've seen it up-close-and-personal. And being Kelly Tough, well, you'll have to continue reading to understand what that really means and why it just might matter to you and your story.

What you're about to read is a love story.

A love between a father and his daughter.

And a greater love between your heavenly Father and you.

Yes, you.

If this were just my story then I'd suggest you set this book down now and let it collect dust on your nightstand or bookcase shelf. Like my story, there's more to your story than you ever imagined or dreamed possible. Maybe just the thought of that seems impossible, especially now in the midst of what you're going through. But whatever circumstance or heartbreak you find yourself overwhelmed by right now, I promise you that it's not the end of the story.

In fact, it just might be one of the greatest chapters of your life. You might not see it or believe it now, but someday you will. And maybe that someday will be the day you read the last page of this book. Because as I already mentioned, this isn't just my story; it's yours too.

One quick thing before we move on. At the end of each chapter I share what I have called "by faith," a summary of sorts for you to ponder as well as a few quotes and some verses I really like from the Bible that I feel compliment the content shared in the chapters.

Like I said in the beginning, I'd rather this book didn't exist. But now that it does, I am so thankful for all that God has done in the midst of these pages. I trust that He will do a work in your life from the moment you lift the cover until the time it is placed back on the shelf or into someone else's hands.

With love,

Erin

P.S. For the sake of continuity and a better reading experience, and since I teamed up with my mother to write this book, there are a few moments that we decided to share in chapter 6 where I was not present to experience, but my mother was. She shared with me the details of what happened, and rather than explain these moments through her voice, we decided to keep them in mine. The funny thing is, after she told me about them, I felt the same way she did. Like mother, like daughter.

This was done, and recorded, in order to encourage God's people in all ages to trust Him in the greatest straits.

—Matthew Henry

Sometimes the victory isn't in the winning or the losing, but in the willingness to join the fight regardless of the odds, or the fear.

PROLOGUE

The distance that divided us stood like a towering wall between me and the hug I ached to give my dad.

A gray and grim sky shrouded Jerusalem, ushering in a cold and dreary day that cast a sullen damper on our trip. It was Friday, March 14, 2014, spring break my freshman year at Liberty University. Mom and I were on a study tour in Israel with a group of students and their parents. We were only able to use our phones for a short time during the day, and with the time change being so significant, the window to communicate with family back home was brief at best.

Our guide had just led us into what was thought to be the place where Pontius Pilate confronted Jesus. As we made our way with the group over to where a presentation would soon begin, my mom felt her phone vibrate. Reaching into her jacket pocket, she pulled it out and peered into the screen. "That's weird. Uncle Danny is calling me," she murmured, pivoting to step away and answer the call. She waved me on to continue with the group. I wanted to hear what our guide had to say, but I was distracted and concerned. I knew my dad's younger brother, Uncle Danny, wasn't calling to just say hi. Hanging toward the back of the group, I kept an eye on my mom while trying to politely eavesdrop on her conversation. Fear-filled thoughts raced through my mind as a growing sense of dread cast a shadow over my heart. *Why is Uncle Danny calling?* I wondered uneasily. *Something must be wrong back home for him to call us. He knows we're in Israel.*

At this point, the only presentation I was listening to was my mother's as my anxiety began to bourgeon into alarm. I continued to wonder, worry, and watch as she moved over to a private space and stood in the corner. By the look on her face and the way she shifted her gait in circles, I knew something was wrong. Uncle Danny wouldn't have called us unless it was serious, and her body language had me thinking the worst.

Almost a year before our trip, my dad had been diagnosed with squamous-cell carcinoma of the upper jawbone. In early June 2013 he had extensive oral surgery to remove the cancer. The doctors said they had gotten all the margins and that Daddy was cancer free. Although he continued to get MRIs and scans after surgery, the doctors were confident that it was gone, and we were banking on what they said. The nightmare was over—or so we thought. Before we left for the Holy Land, my dad had been suffering severe pain in his upper jaw and cheek, but we had no idea why. Unfortunately, Uncle Danny had confirmed what my mom's expression had told me...*the cancer was back!*

The news was shocking, and I was devastated. It's every child's deepest fear. I didn't know how bad it was, how much pain he was in, or what the prognosis was. Yet as hard as it was not knowing, I found peace in that moment knowing that God knew, and I chose to rest in the reality that He loves my father even more than I do. And although I ached to be near my dad, the only way I felt like I could do that was through prayer, even from half a world away.

Our tour group eventually made its way over to what is historically known as the Western Wall or the Wailing Wall. Among the most intriguing tourist attractions in the Holy Land, it is located in the Old City of Jerusalem in the Jewish Quarter, at the foot of what Israel refers to as the Temple Mount. This area, a remnant of the foundation of the second temple from the time of Jesus, is considered the holiest site in Judaism, and the Wailing Wall itself draws multitudes who visit it to pray. With tremendous archeological and religious value, it is regarded as both a secular and sacred treasure that is frequented by tourists and residents alike. Those who come to the Wailing Wall frequently write prayer requests on slips of paper and place them deep in its cracks and crevices. Deeply venerated, portions of the wall are historic remnants of the timeworn barricade that once encircled the temple in ancient days. Thus, it has been the destination of spiritual wayfarers for centuries, captivating pilgrims as far back as the fourth century.

As intrigued as I was with the tour, after hearing the news about my dad, heaviness hung over my heart. It was cold, cloudy, and pouring down rain, and the line to get in trailed far from the entrance. We all huddled under umbrellas in small groups as close to one another as we possibly could while we waited patiently to get in. Although the wait was long, I was distracted. I wanted to talk to Daddy, hear his voice, and just know that he was going to be okay. The struggle to engage in all that was going on around me was brutal. Here I was visiting and studying in one of the most amazing places in the world—the ground where God, the person of Jesus Christ, literally walked and talked, raised the dead, and healed the sick—and all I could think about was my dad.

There were numerous armed guards at the security entrance to get into the Wailing Wall. In order to enter we had to walk through an area that looked very much like what you would see at a security checkpoint in major airports in the United States. All of our belongings were screened, and we each had to walk single file past an interrogation-type table where armed guards stood, each giving us a look that makes you feel guilty of something. It was actually quite scary. You could literally feel the tension and the war between two worlds—light and darkness—driven by the longstanding hatred between the Jews, Christians, and Muslims. The obvious apprehension and uneasiness that overshadowed our group's countenance left no doubt that we were a bunch of American tourists.

Once we made it through security, we didn't have a lot of time, so our guide explained the protocol to follow if we wanted to pray at the wall. Of course, you don't go to the Wailing Wall and not pray. And on this particular day, I had one prayer on my mind and heart—one man who needed the healing that Jesus performed when He had walked where we were thousands of years prior to that very moment. It didn't take me long to grab a pen and rip a piece of paper out of my journal and start writing.

There was great reverence near the wall. A permanent partition separated the wall down the middle where men were allowed to pray on one side and women on the other. With our prayers written down and folded up, my mother and I linked arms and made our way to the wall. I'll never forget how I felt as I stood there almost stunned by the holiness of the moment. For the first few minutes I couldn't help but watch the other women around me. Some were weeping. Some were standing on chairs reaching hands up to the wall to tuck small pieces of paper filled with words of prayer into crevices. Some swayed back and forth and side to side praying in a language I was not familiar with. Some were on their knees, facedown on the ground, literally wailing at the wall. I wondered what lay so heavy on their hearts and what they longed for God to do for them.

My mother and I were silent as we walked away from the wall and the prayers we had tucked into crevices there. Spoken words in the midst of such a deep and holy moment would have robbed us of what God was doing in our hearts. It was unforgettable. Eventually we talked and cried. We both had so much to unload. We shared about how thankful we were that God is not confined to the Wailing Wall.

As holy and amazing as it was to walk up to that wall, pray, and tuck a prayer into a little crevice that over the years has heard and seen countless prayers from people all over the world—as profound an experience as that is and was—God is greater still. He reaches into the deep places in our hearts where only He can go. He sees us wailing at the wall of our own choosing: the walls of fear, doubt, unforgiveness, religion, pride. Walls we build up in order to protect ourselves. Walls that ultimately confine and enslave us.

I knew that even though in that moment my dad and I were separated by a wall thousands of miles wide, so much greater than both of us, it was not greater than God and what He was going to do in the midst of our circumstances.

As soon as we were back in the United States, and I mean literally the moment we landed on American soil, both my mother's phone and mine were inundated with voice messages, texts, tweets, and Facebook comments regarding Daddy's health. It was all over social media, as well as local and national news. I was comforted by the sincere love and prayer support we were receiving, and at the same time it was heart-wrenching to hear the word "cancer" spoken in the same breath as my father's name yet again.

But I was born a Kelly. And as I sat there, I realized that I could run from the waiting battle, or run to it—I had a choice to make. We all do. Sometimes it's in the midst of the battle when we have to remember the victories we've already won, the people who stood by us along the way, and how we made it and triumphed despite the odds stacked against us. And sometimes the victory isn't in the winning or the losing, but in the willingness to join the fight regardless of the odds, or the fear—because it's the right thing to do. And in doing so, I'm convinced you come out victorious, even if you lose a few battles along the way.

Being Kelly Tough means you always do more than what's expected of you. To go the extra mile when you're exhausted. To give and keep giving when you feel like you can't give anymore. To play through the pain, and go above and beyond—without being told.

○ ○ ○

Chapter 1

GROWING UP KELLY

y dad wanted me to be a boy.

I can't say that I blame him. When you grow up in a family with five brothers, like my dad did, there's a bit of testosterone overload. At the time my mom was pregnant with me, boys had already been born to three of my dad's brothers. Uncle Ed was the only brother who had a daughter.

The Kelly brothers are all about being just that: brothers. So you can imagine the anticipation for my father's firstborn. It was fierce. I'm pretty sure everyone just assumed I would be a boy—no question about it. Jim Kelly? Of course his firstborn will be a boy. My quarterback position was already reserved on the roster with the #12 stitched into my jersey. I was the unforeseen firstborn, a surprise gift wrapped in NFL expectations, the one who would hopefully carry on the Kelly name and legacy. To everyone's surprise, however, rather than having his protégé quarterback, my dad was instead blessed with a cheerleader.

I was and still am "Daddy's girl"—with no apologies! Although the first words out of my mouth as an infant were "Hi, Jack" (my mom's brother, Uncle Jack, was so proud), the next full sentence I can recall saying was, "Jim Kelly big muscles." To me, Daddy had big muscles. In fact, everything about him was big: his voice, his hands…and his legend!

My dad's hands are massive and strong. I've watched many a football fan walk away grimacing in pain after a meet and greet. Obviously he doesn't mean to squeeze so hard; he's just strong and tough. He's a Kelly, and historically known as the toughest quarterback in the National Football League. Should we expect anything less than a bone-breaking handshake from a guy who can still heave the ball into the next county? It's true: years after hanging up his cleats, my dad can still throw the pigskin to put six points on the scoreboard like any of the NFL quarterback greats today. I've witnessed him do it time and time again at his yearly football camp for kids.

I love watching the new kids at camp see Daddy throw for the first time. Words like "wow" and "oh my" fall out of jaw-dropped mouths. It's a pretty awesome sight. Especially if you're his daughter and you get to stand back and watch the crowd go wild, then whisper to yourself, "That's my dad." He's always ready and willing to teach anyone who's interested how to hold a football correctly in order to sling it sailing through the air. I was heading into kindergarten when I was taught how to grip a football for the first time, and I'll never forget how to do it. "Second finger, second string." Let me explain.

There are strings on a football, laces really, and you put your second finger (otherwise known as your ring finger) on the second string down on the top of the football. I might have to shoot a video clip of daddy doing the Kelly grip because, I admit, trying to describe it so you can visualize it is a bit of a challenge. Anyway, my hand was pretty small when I first learned how to grip a football. However, I will say that I've grown up some and sent many a sweet spiral sailing into the waiting hands of a running receiver, making my dad very proud, to say the least.

I may not be "Jim Kelly big muscles," but I am my dad's daughter! I learned early on the wisdom and joy of doing what he said and striving to meet his expectations. For example, I can't recall when I learned how to look someone in the eye and give a firm handshake but I've been doing it for as long as I can remember—because that's what he taught me to do. "Erin, when I introduce you to someone, you look them in the eye and give a firm handshake," he'd say sternly. And he didn't just tell me once or twice; he made it very clear that that's what Kellys do (and in case it hasn't hit you yet, I realized I was a Kelly at a very young age). It's called respect, and he made sure I understood what it meant and looked like in the most practical way from my most tender years—eye contact and a firm handshake.

Responding with a "Yes, ma'am," or "No, sir," would come later, but that too became very important to my father. Oddly, it must be more of a Southern thing because when I respond that way at home, in Buffalo, people get kind of offended. I'm not sure why, but regardless of whom it may offend, if Daddy wants me to say, "Yes, ma'am," or "No, sir," that's what I'm going to say. He's my father and I both respect him and long to please him.

It's not just my dad's hands that are big; his presence is towering as well. At six foot three, he has some serious swag. Yes, I know that's a twenty-first-century thing and the man's in his mid-fifties, but nonetheless, it's true. You know when my dad walks into a room. I don't know if it's the deep tone in his voice, his stature, distinct stride, all of the above, or something more, but as a little girl, it was almost as if you could feel when he walked into the room before you looked up and saw him.

In a way, I guess I was sort of scared of him because he was so strong and larger than life to me. You could often hear him approach, every step growing louder and more thunderous as he drew near—kind of like a gathering storm blowing in. But other than those moments when I had done something wrong and was getting in trouble for it, I wanted to be with him. I wanted to snuggle up in his lap as often as possible. I couldn't get enough of him. I longed to spend time with my dad when I was little, and I still do.

There are only a few things I remember about my dad during my younger years. He used to read to me, watch cartoons with me, brush my hair, and let me paint his face with makeup and do his hair. Yes, these are the types of things little girls remember. I loved when Daddy would brush my hair. He was always very gentle and would brush and brush until I told him he could stop. And it wasn't just the brushing that I enjoyed; it was those moments just being with him, giggling and talking about the "nothing and everything" that little girls talk about.

Daddy was so good about letting me fiddle with his fine, thin hair. My choice of style was usually at least five or more baby pigtails all around his head. Add some makeup or face paint and he was one handsome dude. Truth is, he was handsome to me, no matter what. In fact, due to hair loss from chemotherapy and radiation, he had to shave his head. And I think he's more handsome now than ever.

I was not a fan of sleeping in my room alone when I was a toddler. In fact, after my brother, Hunter, was born I rarely slept in my room by myself. Whenever my dad put me to bed, he would read to me or we'd watch *Barney and Friends* or *Little Bear* until we both fell asleep. I don't remember the stories he read, but I do remember how animated he was, making every story fun to listen to. And I'm pretty sure he enjoyed watching cartoons more than I did—oh my, how he would laugh at things that were not even

There will always be voices and influences trying to pull you away and distract you from what's good and right. My parents taught me to stand above the fray—to do the right thing because it's the right thing to do.

funny. He was so cute. More than anything during our bedtime routines, I loved how I felt all snuggled up next to him. I felt safe (which is probably why I didn't want him to leave). If he was near, I trusted that all was well in my little world, and I'd be safe in the big unknown, looming beyond what I could understand at the time. I still feel this way. When I'm with him, I know he'll protect me, even take a bullet for me if he has to. He's still my "Jim Kelly big muscles."

It wasn't long before sports, specifically football, were introduced into my world. I don't know how old I was when I initially watched it on television or went to my first Buffalo Bills game, but I'm sure it was before I had any clue that the game of football was pumping through my blood and part of my DNA. I was born in May of 1995 while my dad was still playing, still battling, still giving it all for the team, the sport, the fans, and the city he loved so much. This was after the seventeen AFC playoff games, four consecutive Super Bowl appearances, and five Pro Bowls. After the height of his celebrated career and the many accolades and highs and lows that went along with it, I caught the vision like a forward pass. I just didn't know what it was for a few years.

I don't remember bouncing on my mother's hip at Rich Stadium (now named Ralph Wilson Stadium after Mr. Wilson, the late owner of the Bills) while she and throngs of Kelly family members cheered my daddy and his team on to victory. I also don't remember wearing red-white-and-blue #12 jerseys as a child, but our family photo albums are full of pictures of me sporting #12 from the time I was still nursing and all throughout my childhood. As you can imagine, it would only take a quick glance in my closet today and you wouldn't have to guess what team I cheer for.

The Buffalo Bills have always been and will always be my team. As a little girl and now as an adult, I proudly wear my #12 jersey.

What can I say? I was (and still am) his biggest fan! Although I don't recall watching him play, the stories I've heard my entire life make me feel as though I was a part of that era. Whenever my dad and his former teammates get together, tell war stories and reminisce about the good ole days when the Bills were winning championships and battling in Super Bowls, I'm usually not far away, listening and drinking in all the history and excitement.

As a Kelly, sports were woven into the fabric of my life, kind of like a tapestry. Whether it's playing the game, cheering the Bills on from the sideline, or watching ESPN every morning, sports are part of who I am. They always have been and always will be. My formal introduction to athletics began while I was still cutting teeth. If football would've been a logical choice, my dad would've had me slinging it and running pass routes in the backyard as soon as I could put one foot in front of the other. But girls didn't play football—not even Kelly girls. And I didn't until powder puff league my senior year of high school. And yes, my dad was our coach.

Basketball was Daddy's second choice for me. Believe it or not, my father was better at basketball in high school than he was at playing football—crazy, but true. I was eight years old when I started learning the game of basketball. My neighborhood best friend, Bailey, and I were part of an organized league in town. By this time, Mom was very busy taking care of Hunter and my little sister, Camryn, so Daddy taught me everything he knew about the game. But even more than that, he taught me how to be a team player, how to play with heart and passion, and how to be Kelly Tough and never give up. On the basketball court or in the driveway, Daddy worked me hard and taught me the basics of the game. We would repeat the same drills over and over again until I got them down—or at least until my arms felt like they would fall off.

Basketball was a way for us to connect, spend time together, and have fun—just the two of us. We would stay outside for hours perfecting my form and working on post-up moves. Most days would end with a round of P-I-G or a one-on-one game. There are still tally marks written on the walls of our garage from all the games that he beat me. Although I will say I did win a few games fair and square (and earned every point)!

Daddy trained me during the summer to prepare me for each season. I can still hear him saying, "You don't go to tryouts to get in shape. You go to tryouts in shape. It's not so much what you do on the court that makes you great but what you do when no one is watching." Going into high school I knew I would have to work hard to make varsity my freshman year. It was a summer filled with hard work, sacrifice, and passion-driven tears, but I was determined to make it and my dad was determined to help me get there. Thankfully, I did make the varsity basketball team as a freshman. I have my dad to thank for that. I listened intently to his instructions, hanging on every word he said. I did what I was told and then did more.

Being Kelly Tough means you always do more than what's expected of you. To go the extra mile when you're exhausted. To give and keep giving when you feel like you can't give anymore. To play through the pain, and go above and beyond to help out—without being told. To be the first one to pick up the slack and help a brother or sister in need. Walking in these disciplines demands commitment and determination, a willingness to act alone based upon what is right, honorable, and true rather than the pressure of peers or the crush of circumstances and culture.

There are and always will be voices and influences trying to pull you away and distract you from what's good and right. My parents taught me to stand above the fray, to do the right thing because it's the right thing to do. Not that they got it right every time—they didn't. But through their mistakes and the consequences they have experienced, they have been willing to expose their weaknesses so that I might learn from them and perhaps make wiser choices. It's a way of life that's often hard and costly, but deeply rewarding. And it's in this tradition that one of my more defining moments and radical pursuits while "growing up Kelly" took place.

by faith...

Living with passion and purpose doesn't just happen. It has a cost and demands desire, determination, devotion, and discipline. You have to look for and seize every opportunity to go the extra mile, to play through the pain, to rise above the circumstances, and live beyond yourself if you really want to make a difference. The pursuit of what is right, honorable, and true is costly, but the sacrifice is worth it. None of this is even remotely possible without God's help. We don't have what it takes to live the kind of life that makes a difference in the here and now. But God does. In and through Him, we are able to do the impossible as well as the right thing when it's the right thing to do. Living this kind of life leaves a God-honoring legacy long after we take our last breath.

> Children, obey your parents in the Lord, for this is right. "Honor your father and mother"—which is the first commandment with a promise—"that it may go well with you and that you may enjoy long life on the earth." —Ephesians 6:1–3

> Children, obey your parents in everything, for this pleases the Lord. —Colossians 3:20

Whatever you do, work at it with all your heart, as working for the Lord, not for men, since you know that you will receive an inheritance from the Lord as a reward. It is the Lord Christ you are serving.
—Colossians 3:23–24

For we are God's workmanship, created in Christ Jesus to do good works, which God prepared in advance for us to do. —Ephesians 2:10

Chapter 2

○ ○ ○

HUNTER

Hunter is my little brother and my best friend.

We were twenty-one months apart, and I was the proudest sister on the planet when he was born. On my dad's birthday, Valentine's Day, February 14, 1997, I welcomed my brother into the Kelly family with unbridled anticipation and excitement. Even as a baby, Hunter brought me so much joy. I excitedly clung to my mother's side and watched every move she made as she cared for Hunter, hoping that someday I too would be able to take care of him.

Everything about him seemed perfect. His hair was chestnut brown, soft as silk, and wavy. His eyes were emerald green and they sparkled like stars. I thought he was the most handsome boy I had ever seen. When I looked at his tiny hands and long, chunky fingers, I imagined that someday he would grow to be big and strong, able to throw a football like my dad. But he never did.

I remember that horrible day as if it were yesterday. Grammie had come over to take care of us while my parents went to the doctor's office to talk about Hunter. He had been crying all the time, and no one knew why or how to help him, so the doctor did some blood work to try to figure it all out. As I heard the doorknob turn, I looked up in hopeful anticipation but was stunned by the grim expression my mom and dad both had etched into their faces. It described their meeting with the doctor better than any amount of dialogue ever could, and, even as young as I was, I knew that something terrible had happened, as they slowly trudged through the door.

Mommy's eyes were red and swollen as if she had been crying, and Daddy's expression was rigid and strained—he looked distraught. Grammie asked me to keep an eye on Hunter while she hurried into the kitchen to talk to my parents. As I sat next to him and held his hand, I heard Grammie sternly blurt out, "I don't believe it! I don't believe it!" The atmosphere was upsetting, and I desperately wanted to know what was going on. But at the same time, I was told to take care of my brother, so I tried to focus on him instead of listening to the conversation in the kitchen.

The tension was so thick you could almost see it, leaving me confused and scared. *What's wrong?* Nervous, I covered Hunter with the soft blanket lying next to me on the couch. As Grammie stormed into another room to call the doctor, Mommy came over and gently sat next to Hunter and me. "What's wrong, Mommy? Why are you crying?" I asked, moving my hand up to her face to wipe away the tears streaming down her cheeks. She answered my question with more tears. As Mom picked Hunter up and cradled him in her arms, I snuggled up as close as I could to them and whispered, "Everything's going to be okay, Mommy. Everything's going to be okay." Little did I know that everything wouldn't be okay. Everything would change.

What I could not possibly understand as a toddler, I eventually learned but still could not fully comprehend that my younger brother, the one destined for football greatness, was born with a fatal genetic disease called Krabbe leukodystrophy. (Please visit Appendix A to learn more about my brother, the disease, and how our family fights for and brings hope to children like Hunter.) He would never follow in Daddy's—or anybody's—footsteps. Rather, he made a mark of his own. He paved a way that no healthy man's steps could ever make—footprints that would never be visible to the human eye, but ones that would radically change our view. He would never play hide-and-seek with me. He would never smile, walk, talk, or do what normal healthy boys do. The doctors told us that he would probably not live to see his second birthday. They told Mom and Dad that there was no cure or treatment for Hunter's disease, and the best thing to do was to take him home and make him comfortable until he passed away.

Although the doctors declared that Hunter was disabled or terminally ill, he was the most able and alive person I knew. There was nothing Hunter couldn't do, even though he was powerless to do anything on his own, including the things we naturally take for granted, such as talking, smiling, swallowing, and even blinking. Hunter was Kelly Tough in every way that a Kelly can be tough, and while that exact phrase wasn't used, I actually first heard the idea expressed when my dad referred to Hunter at his NFL Hall of Fame induction ceremony in 2002.

I was just seven years old, but it was a marquee moment I will never forget. In the closing comments of my father's acceptance speech, he passionately proclaimed, "Since the day I was selected, I prayed to God that my son would be here with me today. God has granted me that blessing. It has been written throughout my career that toughness is my trademark. Well, the toughest person I've ever met in my life is my hero, my soldier, my son, Hunter. I love you, buddy."

And though the expression "Kelly Tough" would eventually

find its place in the family and then out in the public arena, it found its place in my heart that day, at that time, in that epic encounter with greatness. Not the greatness celebrated by the pomp and circumstance honoring the HOF Class of '02. Rather, the hallowed hush of a humble little boy, who, with the heart of a lion and a voice that couldn't even whisper, spoke volumes. Those words that were unable to be uttered continue to echo healing and hope to multitudes who will never enjoy the privilege of meeting him.

Despite his immeasurable health challenges, and by the sheer grace of God, we chose to treat Hunter like he was living rather than dying. We took him horseback riding, swimming, sledding, and even snowmobiling. And yes—those expressions of love were a lot of extra work, but love is often a lot of extra, isn't it? These monumental achievements were buried treasures that veiled untold riches beneath the everyday—riches of the great love that God extended to us through Hunter's life.

Hunter and I did everything together. I can't recall a day where I wasn't snuggling next to him watching *Little Bear*, playing Rescue Heroes, or hanging out in the Jacuzzi. Oh, and speaking of Jacuzzis, first let me clarify that what we called a "Jacuzzi" growing up was really a huge bathtub that could fit like four or five of my friends comfortably. It was kind of like a small indoor swimming pool, but not exactly. For me, it was where my brother spent two hours every night. Because of all the Krabbe-related medical complications Hunter dealt with, water therapy was one of the many rehabilitative interventions that helped him. But being in warm water wasn't just a therapeutic exercise for my brother; it was a special time for family fun as well.

I can recall many a time when Mommy, Hunter, and I hid under mounds of bathtub bubbles. Daddy would come walking in with my little sister, Camryn, and they would pretend like they had

I now understand what a gift it is to take care of those who can't take care of themselves. And to give for the pure sake of giving to someone unable to give you anything back in return.

no idea where we were. Then, just when they were about to leave the bathroom, we'd pop up through the bubble mound and yell, "Surprise!" Of course that would usually lead to a very messy and wet bathroom floor and a little sister who tried climbing into the bathtub fully clothed. I'm laughing now thinking about all the fun we used to have. Hunter's daily tub time turned out to be a necessity that became one of the most cherished activities of the day.

One Jacuzzi jaunt in particular was not only fun for me as usual, but also life changing. For as long as I live, I will never forget this defining moment. I was just five years old. Grammie was spending the night so that Mommy could get some much-needed rest. Actually, my grandmother was always there with us to help with Hunter's nonstop needs, taking turns caring for him during the night because he needed medications, chest therapy, and a whole roster of medical interventions.

Wanting to get in on all the bath-time fun, I got my bathing suit on, walked up to the edge of the tub, and just smiled at Grammie. She knew what I wanted and, in her loving and gracious way, she smiled and said, "Come on in, Erin Marie." It was during that particular "Jacuzzi time" with Hunter and Grammie that the extraordinary intruded into the everyday, and I made the youthful, but soul-deep decision to ask God to come into my life. (Obviously, I now have a greater understanding of what it means to ask Jesus into your life. I'd like to share more about that with you, so please check out Appendix B.)

The years have obscured the details, adding a haze of ambiguity to what was said and how I felt that night. What I can describe, however, is all that came forth from that life-defining moment and how it has shaped my character, values, and pretty much everything about who I am. My mom and Grammie became Christians about a year and a half after Hunter was born. My mother will tell you unapologetically that after my brother was diagnosed with a fatal disease and everything in her life fell apart, she ran hard after God for selfish reasons. She wanted heaven because she believed Hunter was going there, and although she had no idea what that meant, she wanted it with every fiber of her being. At the time, it wasn't because heaven is all about Jesus, or even paradise, but because her only son, Hunter, was heading there and, as his mama, she wanted to be with him.

Thankfully, God in His indescribable grace and mercy is and was big enough to use the mixed motives of my mother's selfish pursuit of heaven to open her eyes to the Creator of heaven and His love for her and Hunter. While my mother was desperately searching for hope and heaven and how to get there, my grand-mother was desperately praying for Hunter's healing. Heaven and healing were the motivation, but eventually the two most amazing women I know found the reason for the only hope that they had (and still have) in the midst of their deepest heartbreak—Jesus.

So consequently, as a young girl, I grew up in what you would call a Christian home. (Although I will add that my dad did not become a believer until about a year or so after my brother went to heaven.) Day after day, for the first ten years of my life, I watched my mother and grandmother put one foot in front of the other to take care of Hunter's every need, every day, round the clock. This was our "normal"! I was awestruck and wanted to be just like them, so much so that I would pretend my baby dolls had Krabbe disease like Hunter, and I would go through the same protocols that I watched them perform with my brother. I thought I had perfected it and could take care of Hunter just like they did.

Through word and deed, these two women helped point me to the life and sacrifice of the only One worthy of my very life. Their guidance, discipline, and steadfast love helped mold and shape me into the woman of faith I am today. I've watched them cry, pray, praise, and seek hard after the Lord, and although I didn't understand the fullness of my decision then, I knew I wanted what they had. And I still do!

In the years that followed my bathtub confession of faith, and as Hunter's health continued to deteriorate, I began to seek the Lord. Loving Him was a necessity but also a privilege. Camryn and I wanted to be as much a part of everything as we could, so we stayed with them in the upper part of the master bedroom where my mom and Hunter were.

Every night I fell asleep to the melodic sound of Hunter's suction machine, oxygen tank, or chest therapy, and yet, I wouldn't have wanted it any other way. To be honest, after he was gone and there was no need for the machines, it took a long time to get used to the deafening silence. It was too quiet, too still—an intimidating, cheerless, and empty hush that assailed my ears and echoed through my heart. Even now, all these years later, there are times when I ache to hear those special Hunter noises again, because I still ache to be near Hunter.

One night I climbed into bed next to my mom as Hunter slept peacefully to her left and seized the opportunity to tell her about the one thing I longed to do with my little brother. Camryn was already asleep back in our bed, so I snuggled in and whispered, "Mommy, can I sleep with Hunter one night and take care of him?" Her tired eyes opened slightly and a sweet, sleepy smile made its way to her face as she quickly assured me that one night I would be able to.

I ran and bounded back in bed with an unexplainable excitement, delighted that I would be able to sleep by Hunter's side through the night, being there to take care of his every need. The blankets felt as warm and cozy as the joy I curled up in, wrapped up in the new anticipation I embraced. Joy because of the boy who radiated Jesus so profoundly that being near him somehow made me feel deeply loved and close to God.

I've never met anyone else who could spread joy like my brother, and he did it without being able to crack a smile, speak a word, or reach out to hug me. And it wasn't just joy he radiated, but love. Hunter was never able to say the words "I love you," but I knew he did. Not because he was my brother or because he could blink three times, which meant, "I love you," but because the love of God flowed out of him. You could feel it just being in the same room as Hunter. It was never about Hunter showing us love; it was about him being filled with God's love and living to make His extraordinary love known.

* * *

August 8, 2005—the worst day of my life…I pushed myself out of the car as tears filled my eyes in the helpless realization that my one and only request would never be fulfilled. I'll never forget the moment. We had just arrived home from Hunter's funeral and burial service and I was completely heartbroken, shattered, frustrated, and sad. Before I got out of the car I looked at my mom with tears streaming down my face and stammered, "I never got to sleep with Hunter and take care of him like you promised." And without another word I stormed into the house.

Our house didn't feel like home without Hunter; it felt empty and cold. I missed my brother and everything about him. His wavy brown hair, his deep green eyes, his adorable angelic face, and soft skin. He was perfect. Regardless of every machine and medication he needed, I saw nothing more and nothing less than the radiance and love of God through Hunter.

Although I spent most of my time with him, after he was gone,

That's when we are all at our strongest—when we're at our weakest, but choose to press on, walk by faith, and trust God no matter what.

I wished I had spent more. I remember weeping tears of deep regret, ashamed that I hadn't spent more time being Hunter's big sister. There was a sense of guilt, but mostly there was just sorrow and remorse over the bitter reality I had no choice but to accept. The reality that my moments spent with Hunter would now only be memories.

Because I never saw Hunter as disabled, I lived life with him to the fullest. He was simply my little brother and he loved me—and I knew it! I lavished love on him, invested in him, and showed him how much he meant to me. And while we are blessed beyond measure to be able to show love, Hunter could only "be" love—and the power in that eclipses even the best everyday expressions of love.

It has been nine years since my hero went to heaven, and I've matured a lot. I've seen death. I've experienced deep sorrow and anguish of heart. Oddly, walking through some of life's raw realities has settled my uneasy heart and mind lately as I've watched my dad struggle through cancer. I believe God has used what I walked through in my innocence and immaturity as a young girl so that even now in the reality of sickness and death, I can live to the fullest with my dad like I did with Hunter.

I was never overcome with the fear of losing Hunter because I lived in the moment and didn't even consider the thought that one day I might lose him. Or that one day I might walk through the front door from school and not be able to hug and kiss him. But in the midst of my dad's battle, I've grappled with an immense fear of losing the man who, God-willing, will one day walk me down the aisle. It's the kind of fear that keeps you up at night and makes your mind wander from reality. A fear that grips you so savagely that it physically hurts.

Since my father had a feeding tube placed in his body, I've helped him get his food ready numerous times. And as I type this sentence right now, he still has his feeding tube and we're not sure exactly when they'll be able to take it out. He's lost over sixty pounds as a result of the cancer and treatment side effects. He still has a lot of pain in his oral and sinus cavity due to the radiation and chemotherapy, and the doctors aren't sure how long the pain will last or when he will be able to eat a sufficient amount of food to sustain his diet.

Regardless, for as long as he has that tube, or for as long as he's here, alive, I'm going to take care of him. Maybe it's because I long to show him love in any and every way possible. Maybe it's because I've watched, learned, listened, and now understand what a gift it is to take care of those who can't take care of themselves. And to *give* for the pure, unadulterated sake of giving to someone unable to give you anything back in return.

Maybe, I just miss my brother and wish that I could've done more to help take care of him. What I wouldn't give to be near him right now. Or maybe it's all of the above—or even something deep within me that I am completely unaware of. Maybe it's as simple and profound as God allowing me to experience the joy and pain of taking care of someone we both love.

There's a verse in the New Testament that I think sums up beautifully what I've just shared: "Truly I tell you, whatever you did for one of the least of these brothers and sisters of mine, you did for me" (Matthew 25:40). The Lord Almighty, architect of the universe, trusts you and me to be His hands and feet. If He wants to embrace a broken heart, He's going to reach through the pain using your arms and mine. If He wants to feed the hungry, dry another's tears, or help the needy, He's going to use our feet to get there. In the end, we can only take *His* healing to the broken-hearted—*His* strength to the weak. Maybe we do that by coming to the end of ourselves through another's weakness so that we might find strength in the One who is greater.

I still don't understand why Hunter had to suffer so much, or why my father has had to suffer through cancer and the difficult aftermath of its treatment. I don't understand why at times God seemed so far away in the midst of moments when we needed desperately to sense His nearness. I sometimes still ask Him why He didn't heal my brother. There are a lot of things I still don't understand. But thank God I don't have to understand everything—it's enough for me that He knows and understands. I continue to learn. I'm still a work in progress. And every day I'm grasping the fact that I can rest in the reality that God knows and still meets me right where I am in the midst of my questions, doubts, and fears. And maybe the reason to all my "whys" is that God was and is revealing His strength and love in the midst of my weakness and the weakness of the two strongest people I know, Hunter and my dad. Maybe it's their physical vulnerability that has allowed me to view them as the toughest individuals on the planet. Because maybe that's when we are all at our strongest—when we're at our weakest, but choose to press on, walk by faith, and trust God no matter what.

by faith...

Life isn't perfect or easy. People you love get sick and die. Things happen that deeply hurt, leaving scars on the outside and even more so on the inside. But God is good. Despite the circumstances and scars of life, God in His infinite, unmatched love and mercy works all things together for our good and His glory. Trusting Him and His sovereignty regardless of how we feel or what we see happening all around us allows us to persevere and press on in the midst of our weaknesses and vulnerability so that we can walk in His power, courage, and strength.

And we know that in all things God works for the good of those who love him, who have been called according to his purpose. —Romans 8:28

And I believe with all my heart that sometimes it is through the lives of those who are mentally or physically challenged, or those bearing up under suffering, that Jesus chooses to shine in the most spectacular ways. —Joni Eareckson Tada[1]

---

[1] Joni Eareckson Tada, *A Place of Healing: Wrestling with the Mysteries of Suffering, Pain, and God's Sovereignty* (Colorado Springs, CO: David C. Cook, 2010), 71.

Chapter 3

○ ○ ○

THE ROOKIE SEASON

My mom and dad weren't married when I was born. In fact, when my mom found out that she was pregnant with me, one of our family members suggested she get an abortion. Throwing touchdown passes was what my father did best, and at that point, starting a family was not in his playbook. Thankfully, my parents chose life and not death for me.

One of the most profound and powerful life skills modeled for me by my parents while growing up Kelly is a triple threat I like to call *admitting when you're wrong, owning your choices, and learning from and making the best of the repercussions and consequences!* I'm still working at it, but trust me when I tell you I am extremely grateful for the example of humility, honesty, and forgiveness my mom and dad have lived out in front of me.

Talk about Kelly Tough, I sometimes think it's way tougher facing the truth about ourselves than facing a 250-pound blitzing linebacker coming at you full speed like my dad did throughout his career! At least on the field you can throw the ball away, but the only option left after you admit what you see in the mirror is to take the hit and hope you don't fumble.

The awesome thing about embracing reality, however, is that God's grace can turn a loss into a gain, a mess into a message, and a test into a testimony. Let me share some of the backstory so you can hopefully grasp the greater blessing and significance in all of this. Consider this to be a "TBT" or throwback—if you're on any sort of social media, you'll know exactly what I'm talking about. If not, what I'm going to do is take you back with me to a moment in time.

The house I grew up in was spacious, comfortable, and actually somewhat unassuming for a celebrity athlete. It boasted a long, shadowy hall that stretched about half its length with the kitchen, dining room, and family room each coming off of it, and my parents' master bedroom at the end. As I mentioned in the previous chapter, circumstances with Hunter and his health care needs led to their bedroom being transformed into everyone's room—except my dad's.

Handsomely framed family photos adorned the shadowy hall walls like a photographic tapestry that told our story frame by frame. Hung with artistic precision, they brightened and brought life to an otherwise dull, gloomy passage. I used to love to stare at them, pretending they would come to life, and even though it's a paradox, each photo was my favorite. But be that as it may, there was one photograph in particular that I'll never forget—it was as if the photo hung upon my heart as it did upon the wall.

It was a beautiful sixteen-by-twenty photograph of my mom holding me, printed on canvas and framed in wood. In the captured moment, I'm a sweet little thing with an overwhelming sense of innocence etched into my fragile features. I have on a beautiful white dress trimmed in satin bows. Frilly lace socks and matching white patent leather shoes completed the ensemble.

My hair was toddler short, parted on the side with bangs pulled over and held in place by a petite white-satin-bow barrette that rounded out my overall look. I have to admit: I looked adorable. Mommy looked absolutely drop-dead gorgeous as she cradled me in her arms. As a little girl I remember peering into that picture and thinking, *Mommy looks so pretty all dressed up in her white dress—like a princess.*

I had no idea back then, or for years to come, that the picture I had admired so much was taken at my parents' wedding. It never even crossed my mind that there was something out of sync about the fact that I was a year and fourteen days old on the day my parents exchanged vows. And so it was for years that I was enamored with this beautiful picture of Mommy in her wedding dress holding me as it adorned the main hallway wall of our home, prominently displayed for all to see without reservation.

And as the years drifted on, I grew up. I listened. I learned. And just as two plus two always equals four, time filled in the blanks about that beautiful picture I loved so much, with some very painful questions and perplexing answers. Ultimately discussions about the birds and the bees transitioned into more sophisticated dialogue, which, in turn, took its place among fairy tales and children's stories, as the stunning reality of how babies were made intruded into my innocent, naïve, and delicate world.

I can't remember how young I was when the shock and awe of how a man and woman coming together as one was explained to me. I only recall that it was Mommy who explained it all, and when she was done recounting what can only be described as a "mixed blessing," I was definitely a little older. She read a book to me filled with colorful drawings of boys and girls, and mommies and daddies, and how God made our bodies a special way to come together kind of like puzzle pieces.

The nudity in the book made me feel uncomfortable and awkward, causing all sorts of confusion. I can't help but laugh now

Being Kelly Tough
means admitting
when you're wrong,
owning your choices,
and learning from
and making the best
of the consequences!

about the shock of it all and how hard it must have been for my mom. In classic mommy style, she handled my barrage of questions with love, grace, and a gentle strength. However, I came away from our "sex talk" with deep heart ponderings. For a long time I never shared how I felt or the many questions I had with anyone but God. And the one question that echoed like an image in a hall of mirrors focused on my treasured photograph hanging in the hallway. *If God's plan is that mommies and daddies don't have babies until after they're married, then why is my mom holding me at her wedding?* This bothered me—a lot.

It wasn't that I was angry with my parents; I loved and respected them so much that they could do no wrong in my eyes. I guess I just had a hard time understanding how having me before they were married was bad since I thought they were so good. I was seriously conflicted with my heart pulling me in one direction and my mind pulling me in the other!

Eventually, my mother and I had the talk—the talk I needed to have in order to help me understand what my heart and mind had been wrestling with for so long. It was late one night after my brother, Hunter, was snuggled up in bed sleeping next to Mommy. She motioned for me to hop up in bed next to her, and so I did.

After getting all cozied up and warm under the comforter, Mommy grabbed a magazine sitting on the nightstand next to us. Miley Cyrus was on the cover. The Miley on the cover of that magazine is not the same Miley we see today. Thankfully, the young girl who was all snuggled up next to her mom that night is not the same girl today either. I was excited when my mother opened the magazine and started reading about the girl I thought I wanted to be like. This sounds crazy considering the way Miley has chosen to live her life these days. However, when I was a preteen she was young, fun, and pretty—much the epitome of what most impressionable girls wanted to be like.

What can I say? I was a huge Hannah Montana fan (kids born in the mid-to-late 1990s who loved the Disney Channel will get this), so hearing about her parents' situation and how similar it was to mine ended up connecting with me in a way I desperately needed. God certainly does work in mysterious ways, using anyone and anything to get His point across.

Anyway, Mom shared with me how, like Miley's parents, she and Daddy chose to have sex before marriage. She went on to explain how neither of them knew when they were dating and then living together that God had a more perfect plan. Obviously, I can't remember everything she said that night, but I do recall that somehow I was able to identify with Miley. (I readily admit that it is downright scary how deeply celebrities impact our hearts, minds, virtues, and values. I plan to be more diligent in guarding my children from this someday.)

I also remember that Mom wanted to make certain that I understood that God created sex as a beautiful gift for a man and a woman within the commitment and protection of marriage. It was a lot to absorb at the time, and, in fact, I'm still learning.

Interestingly enough, I would find out years later that my grandma and grandpa, my mom's parents, did the same thing my parents did, with the only difference being that they chose to get married before my mother was born for the sake of saving face, avoiding shame, and "doing the right thing."

Upon discovering that my grandmother and mother had both gotten pregnant before they were married or had surrendered their lives to the Lord, and coming to understand that God had a greater plan, it hit me that there was a generational pattern in our family that needed to be broken. There was also the reality that I was (and still am) part of a culture that encouraged sex outside of marriage, as well as other risky behaviors that made intimacy anything but intimate. I didn't want that for myself, my friends, or my family—it just defied common sense and yet, I'm as human as the next girl.

Movies, music, books, fads, and sports, along with their accompanying heroes, seemed to form an alliance that endorsed a sexual way of thinking and living, which was unthinkable to me. And though I may have only been in my early teens, I simply had a sense of what was right for me. I knew the bait in that trap looked pretty darn good, so I'd be better off thinking about it and drawing my lines ahead of time!

Unlike my mother or grandmother when they were my age, I had a deep relationship with the Lord and sincerely wanted to please Him. Even though I didn't fully comprehend what that meant or what it was supposed to look like lived out every day, my heart's desire was to live for God. And while I may have been sorting out my understanding of morality at the time, I was quickly coming to understand that God had a more beautiful plan for my life.

Make no mistake about it: God has radically and graciously redeemed the choices my parents and grandparents made. It's a blessing to be saved out of something, but even more so to be saved *from* it! So as I considered the road up ahead, I realized it would get harder before it got easier, and so I searched for ways to help me stay true to what I knew in my heart. So I put my faith in motion and decided to do something to seal my convictions, something that would move me in a direction that would help ensure personal accountability and integrity while strengthening my own moral purity.

* * *

I'll never forget that day.

It was an unusually warm spring afternoon and my thirteenth birthday. The vast blue sky was cloudless and beautiful as it stretched over us. Ready or not, I was a teenager. I was something else too—old enough to make a profound decision that would set me in sharp contrast with most of my generation as well as the culture I was growing up in. It was a decision I did not take lightly, a commitment that demanded resolve and endurance—it was a difficult promise to make, and an even more difficult promise to keep.

In light of all that I had learned about my parents and grandparents, and all that I had learned about God, my faith led me to a ceremony that expressed a personal, deeply-held conviction. I knew I was in for a radical ride, but honestly, peer pressure didn't intimidate me all that much. I was more concerned about pleasing God than pleasing my friends. Truthfully, I can't take any credit for this boldness; it was and still is a work of God.

Consequently, with my turbulent teens dead ahead, I wanted to make it clear to God, my parents, my family, and my peers that I was committed to remaining pure until marriage. I felt that sex was a gift, something to cherish, and regarding it as anything but would demean its worth. Consequently, my virginity held tremendous value—it was (and is) a priceless treasure, something that can only be given once to the right person. And I decided in my heart to surrender it to God and my future husband—even though I don't know who he is yet.

Honestly, I have had conversations with some of my closest friends who are no longer virgins, and they all wish they had waited. Sex is a beautiful gift from God reserved for you and your spouse. And my choice to wait and give that gift to my husband isn't just something I'm going to do. It is who I am.

So on my thirteenth birthday, the day God chose to bring

me into this world, I decided to memorialize my commitment to remain sexually pure. And with all that I knew and understood at that time, I meant it! I was going to publicly make vows before God and the people who meant the most to me. I wanted to go past the point of no return with no turning back, treating my sexual purity as the treasure it was and still is.

There was no denying that I was swimming upstream, though, because in most television shows, movies, books, magazines, websites, music—pick a media—you'll most likely find this treasure treated like trash, as if it has little value or consequence. However, my hope and desire was that when I finally did embrace a sexual relationship, it would be with my husband as a beautiful act of love, just as God intended—pleasing to Him and blessed by Him. It may have been a lot for a thirteen-year-old to comprehend completely, but it was well worth celebrating!

The prayer chapel was filled with the most important people in my life. All of my grandparents were there minus Grandma Kelly, who had gone to heaven a month before my parents were married. Mommy's only sibling, Uncle Jack, and his wife, Aunt Kim, along with their three children (my cousins, Benjamin, Paige, and Bradley), were seated up front near my godmother, Mary. Daddy's younger brother, Uncle Danny, and Aunt Kathleen brought their bundle of kids. Also present were a few other special people I had handpicked to witness what would end up being one of the most impactful days of my life.

Pastor Rich had taken his place at the altar in the front of the chapel, while Daddy and I were standing in the back of the room holding hands. I was so nervous. Mom pressed play on her iPod and "My Little Girl," a chart topper by country music superstar Tim McGraw (one of my dad's close friends), tugged at everyone's heartstrings as it played softly in the background.

It was the perfect song to accompany us as we walked down the aisle to where Pastor Rich waited. Daddy put his right arm out for me to link arms with him, and then we started toward the front of the altar. Everyone was smiling, and although I was nervous, I felt happy and secure walking with my dad. When we reached the altar, my mother shut the music off and quickly made her way to the front of the chapel where she sat down in the front pew next to Camryn and Grammie.

The ceremony was poignant and heartwarming, including a very touching and intimate prayer and readings by my sister, Camryn, and my mother and father. After Pastor Rich shared a few Bible verses with us, Daddy pulled a beautiful heart-shaped diamond solitaire ring out of his pocket. He gently slipped it on the ring finger of my right hand. I still wear it today as a symbol of the commitment I made to my earthly father, my future husband, and, most importantly, to my heavenly Father. It holds such a deep and profound meaning that I'm not even sure I really grasp the fullness of it at this point in my life. In fact, I probably won't understand the scope of its meaning until the day I walk down the aisle with my dad again when he gives me away to the man I will spend the rest of my life with.

Tears welled up in both my parents' eyes as I made a commitment to God and my family to remain sexually pure until marriage. Little did I know then the magnitude of what those tears meant. Joy. Pain. Or maybe both.... But the vows that brought those tears mean as much or more to me now as they did when I first spoke them. And they continue to resonate with conviction in my heart to this day.

I share this experience because it's part of my life story, part of growing up Kelly, part of what it means to be Kelly Tough. Making a pledge to remain pure when I was thirteen years old would've been

The awesome thing about embracing reality is that God's grace can turn a loss into a gain, a mess into a message, and a test into a testimony.

a big deal under the most mundane circumstances, but considering the choices my parents and grandparents made, this commitment carried with it an even greater sense of redemption and purpose.

I've heard my mother share her testimony of faith on a number of occasions. When she talks about me being born before she and my dad were married, she always sums it up by saying something like this:

I knew that eventually I would have to tell Erin about the choices Jim and I had made. She was a very smart little girl and I figured it was only a matter of time until she would start asking questions. For years I prayed that God would prepare both of us— her heart to receive the truth and mine to extend it in such a way that she would find freedom through it, because ultimately it's the truth that sets us free.

And as compelling as testimonies like this are, it's only by His grace and because I have been set free that I am motivated to keep my virginity, and, in due course and God-willing, hold up a wedding photograph of my husband and myself on our wedding day—just the two of us. And as I do, I will share a testimony that glorifies God, not for delivering me through the same choices my parents and grandparents made, but by His mercy, keeping me from them.

I don't fault my parents or grandparents for the choices they made. We live in an imperfect world full of imperfect people, who make imperfect decisions, and reap imperfect consequences—all of which can be perfectly redeemed by a perfect God, through His perfect love. We all choose our own way rather than God's way, don't we? But even so, God in His uncompromising goodness and mercy makes a choice too—to take all the pieces of the broken things in our lives and make something more beautiful than we could ever hope for or imagine. He somehow takes it all and works it together for His glory and our good.

by faith...

It's true—we all have baggage and issues and things we don't like to talk about or admit. Yet, in spite of our mistakes and imperfections, our lives can be redeemed and made whole by a perfect God. Based upon His character and through His love, God is committed to finishing the good work He started in all of our lives. Included in this good work are the many ways in which God chooses to use our mistakes and the mistakes of others. Admitting when we're wrong, owning up to our choices, and coming to God in our weakness unleashes His goodness and strength in every area of our lives. And, as a result, we can live in a freedom that breeds forgiveness, authenticity, and so much more.

...for it is God who works in you to will and to act according to his good pleasure. —Philippians 2:13

You were taught, with regard to your former way of life, to put off your old self, which is being corrupted by its deceitful desires; to be made new in the attitude of your mind; and to put on the new self, created to be like God in true righteousness and holiness. —Ephesians 4:22–24

Be very careful, then, how you live—not as unwise but as wise, making the most of every opportunity, because the days are evil. —Ephesians 5:15

It is God's will that you should be sanctified: that you should avoid sexual immorality; that each of you should learn to control his own body in a way that is holy and honorable, not in passionate lust like the heathen, who do not know God.... For God did not call us to be impure, but to live a holy life. —1 Thessalonians 4:3–5, 7

Chapter 4

○ ○ ○

LOVE YOU MORE

Love is not what I thought it was.

It's not the warm and fuzzy heart-pounding feeling we're told it is. It's not what we see portrayed in chick flicks, on *The Bachelorette*, or in Disney fairy tales. It's not the typical three-word sentence written in Valentine cards. It can't be found, bought, or even felt. It didn't take me long to learn that love is not at all what the world and our culture feed us—people don't always live happily ever after.

While growing up I often heard my parents tell one another that they loved each other—they told my siblings and me daily, and they still tell us to this day. Sometimes we don't say, "I love you," to each other but instead we just say, "more," and that communicates that we love each other more than whatever the most love is.

My family and extended family are very affectionate, which basically means we hug a lot. I'm used to it now, but watching my mom meet some of my college friends for the first time has been a bit of comic relief. She automatically hugs people—she can't help it. And I suppose if you don't come from a family that is demonstratively affectionate, it might catch you off guard. In fact, my dad and I still cuddle, and it's often that you'll find me sitting on his lap, because, well, I'll always be his little girl. Because I attend college in another state, the time we are able to spend together is something we both treasure. When it's just the two of us, it doesn't even matter what's going on around me, it's all about just being with him.

In a very real way, love is about value and the way you show this to the people who have the most value to you. Like anything, if it's worth a lot, you'll make the sacrifice to pay for it, and so we are usually willing to invest sacrificially in the lives of those we love. I have been very fortunate to grow up with powerful examples of love through sacrifice on many fronts: first, through watching my mother and grandmother take care of my brother, often very sacrificially; through Hunter's suffering, silence, and humility; and through my family doing all they can to advocate and care for special-needs children through our foundation and its many facets. Most recently, I've watched the love my parents share in the midst of walking through the valley of the shadow of death during my dad's cancer battle.

My parents have been through a lot. In fact, the circumstances they've had to endure probably should have ended their marriage. But they're still together. And I believe their love is stronger than it's ever been, maybe even because of the storms they've weathered. Why do I think that? Well, let me share some of the moments that have convinced me.

It was May 17, 2014, the day before my parents' eighteenth wedding anniversary, and my mom had a crazy idea. My sister, Camryn, Mom, and I had just left the hospital where my dad was going through his radiation treatments. He had to be in the hospital because he had a feeding tube put in since he could no longer sustain his diet through eating by mouth, and he was still dealing with a lot of pain that necessitated medications that he couldn't take at home. We were pulling out of the hospital parking lot when Mom said, "I'm going to wear my wedding dress to the hospital to surprise Daddy tomorrow for our anniversary."

"Mom, are you crazy? Do you even know where your dress is?" Camryn responded. "Will it fit you?" She laughed. My initial thought after Cam chimed in with her typical comments was, *She's definitely crazy, but that's so adorable, and Daddy will love it!* The ride home was spent planning the anniversary surprise, a blessing that would prove to be an unforgettable and defining moment during the most difficult days our family walked through with my dad.

When you marry an NFL quarterback, you wear a stunning wedding dress. My mother's dress was so beautiful that it was featured in the February 10, 1997, issue of *People* magazine as one of the top-ten wedding dresses of the year. When we finally got home from the hospital, Mommy started searching for her dress, all three perfectly preserved pieces of it. Her description of the dress: "The gown, elaborately handmade by Italian designer Pino Lanchetti, consisted of three separate pieces of Italian silk, tulle, and lace; a strapless silk crepe sheath; and a long-sleeved white lace overlay complete with sixty-seven individual buttons down the back and a detachable silk tulle overskirt."

I wouldn't know a silk crepe sheath from a burlap sack, but I do know that her dress was valuable, beautiful, and she looked amazing in it. I know this because of the sixteen-by-twenty framed picture of us that used to hang in the main hallway of our home. It's the same photo I mentioned in the previous chapter of my mother holding me at her wedding—the one that used to stop me in my tracks as a young girl just so I could gaze upon its beauty.

The kind of love
I have witnessed
through my parents
is a selfless love that
sows commitment
against all odds,
inconvenience, and
even pain, which
reaps action, not just
hollow sentiment.
It's a love that is as
it does and is rooted
in something greater
than everything and
anything this world
has to offer.

After searching under beds, in storage, and ransacking closets all over the house, we finally found the dress. Unfortunately, only one of the three pieces from the original wedding dress was in the box—the detachable tulle overskirt. It was the same piece that my mom wore when she and my dad renewed their wedding vows— which is another amazing story of God's grace. I suppose it was a good thing that the overskirt was the piece we unearthed since the other two pieces probably wouldn't have fit her anyway. She was very thin when she got married. But I will say, three kids later, in her mid-forties, she's still rockin it.

With two of the main pieces of the original dress missing, my mom had to find something to wear as a replacement, some- thing that would work with a wedding dress. She also figured that with all Daddy's concussions and now "chemo brain," he probably wouldn't know the difference anyway. After finding the perfect white dress substitute to compliment the original silk tulle over- skirt (check out the photo insert), we started planning the details of the surprise.

"When I surprise Daddy, what if I play our wedding song, the one we danced to at the reception, when he sees me? Whaddaya think?" Mom excitedly asked Cam and me. "That's perfect!" I blurted out. "Yes!" Of course, my sister and I had never heard of the artist Sade or their wedding's first dance song, "Kiss of Life." But when she downloaded it onto her phone and pressed play, you could tell by the joy written all over her face that the song meant a lot to her. She closed her eyes and started dancing around the living room while Cam and I just watched and smiled.

We were up late preparing and planning in order to make this day a sheer inspiration—and maybe spark some much-needed life into my father. The final touch to the surprise was a rectangle sign that read "Love You More." Mommy decided she would carry the sign as she walked down the hospital hallway toward Daddy. It was perfect in every way. "Love you more" is something the four of us say to each other all the time, but even more so these past few months. Those three words carried even deeper meaning to every one of us, especially on days when we found ourselves stretched by very difficult circumstances; the days when all Daddy did was vomit because of the chemo's side effects; or when tears were flowing more than words were spoken because the doctors shared more bad news with us.

After we arrived at the hospital, we made our way up to Daddy's floor and into the nearest bathroom so that Mommy could put on her dress. I'm laughing as I share this because we were stopped by security and asked a barrage of questions due to the huge mound of wedding dress my mother carried into the building. I'm sure it's not every day that you see a woman walk into the hospital carrying a wedding dress. But, there's no one like my mom. She's learned through great heartache and pain that love sometimes does the ridiculous, the undignified, and outrageous; things that only make sense to the one extending love in its various forms.

My grandparents, along with my mom's brother and his family, were all in on the surprise. The plan was for them to go into my dad's room and get him up out of bed for some exercise then walk him down to the end of the hallway. From there, it led to another hallway where my mom would be waiting in her wedding dress. Often, the best plans can unravel unexpectedly, and that's exactly what happened. Thankfully, in the case of the wedding dress surprise, however, everything actually fell into place even better than we had hoped.

Daddy was in the middle of a meeting with Uncle Danny and Mr. Russ Brandon from the Buffalo Bills. Side note: while my dad was going through treatments and fighting cancer, the beloved owner of the Buffalo Bills franchise, Mr. Ralph Wilson, died. New ownership of the team was up for grabs to the highest bidder, and diehard fans were nothing short of freaking out because of fear that a new owner would move the team out of Buffalo. Even though my dad was basically fighting for his life, he loves Buffalo, the Bills, and the fans, and he wasn't about to let anyone come in and steal part of the heart and soul of the city away. Consequently, in the midst of chemo, radiation, feeding tubes, procedures, and pain, he was doing everything he could in his power to make certain the Bills stayed in Buffalo.

Thus, while he was distracted talking football, we slipped into the hallway bathroom while we waited for their meeting to end. Once it did, Daddy unexpectedly decided to walk with Uncle Dan and Russ down the hall. Of course, that's not what we had planned, so we had to quickly finesse an alternative surprise. As they approached the end of the hall where it splits, my grandparents, Uncle Jack, and his family were there waiting. When Daddy got to them, they all said their hellos and hugged, and then he was tactfully ushered to his left where my mother stood just down the hall a bit. After she started to play their wedding song and walk toward him, Daddy turned and saw her.

The look on his face was priceless. "You've got to be kidding me," he blurted out, smiling as he bent over and held his stomach. He had just had his feeding tube put in and was still very sore from surgery, so laughing was somewhat painful. But not for long as the beauty of the moment swept in like rain to a thirsty land, bringing with it some much-needed joy and laughter. That's when I knew their love was so much more than I had thought it was—a love beyond words. I watched my mother invest sacrificially because she wanted my father to actually experience how much he meant to her. She went above and beyond, doing what might be considered crazy or ridiculous to live out the meaning of the words "I love you." I have to say Daddy got the message!

My mom isn't the only one who has lived love—though my father is a bit more spontaneous. Maybe it's from all those years of scrambling away from blitzing linebackers and putting points on the scoreboard on the run. Whatever moves him, my dad knows how to call football plays and make mundane moments seem magical. One of those moments would be another romantic hospital room gesture when Daddy reached out his hand to Mommy and they started slow dancing.

The fact is that everything was working against a dreamy mood: the light was glaring and intrusive, and the only sounds were the gravelly crackle of the hospital loudspeaker and the annoying beeping of the medical equipment my dad was hooked up to. And by the way, said medical equipment was very "leashlike"—not exactly conducive to dancing. There was no music playing to set the mood, and Daddy's feeding tube didn't exactly inspire the thought of a romantic toast. But it didn't matter to my parents. Being able to hold each other, even if only for a moment, produced sparks that inspired an expression of their love for one another that dominated their environment. Reaching for my mother's hand to dance with her set off its own chain reaction—a warmth that touched everyone and everything around it. Maybe it doesn't seem like much, but the little things only appear little, when really they aren't little at all.

The two moments I just shared were lighthearted and tender, exemplifying a love I had never witnessed between my parents. But there were many more moments—too many to count—when I witnessed tears of sorrow, brokenness, and deep anguish; Kelly Tough kind of moments when I watched my mother take care of

We cannot know love unless we know God. And we cannot know God unless we have been drawn to Him through His Son, Jesus, by the power and work of the Holy Spirit.

my dad and then disappear into another room where, after peeking through the cracked open door, I saw her facedown on the floor weeping and praying. And of course there's been many a time when it appeared that love was absent between my parents, and yet there was a greater love in the midst of their mess that was holding all the broken pieces of their marriage and lives together.

There's an old saying that goes, "Love is as love does," meaning, in effect, that if you love someone or even something, you'll act like it—your conduct will reflect your love. Take football, for example. If you love the game you won't blow off practice; in fact, it's very likely that you'll show up early. You'll know the playbook, the positions, the game plan, the opposing team—all of it, because you *love* the game. The same is true of people; you can usually tell if a person has a crush on someone by the way he or she acts toward the other. Certainly, you can tell if a man loves his wife and kids by the way he treats them!

Just watch the guy. If he sacrifices for his family, does without so they can have what they need and want, then there's a good chance that they mean an awful lot to him. It's the kind of love that's based upon his commitment to his family's highest good—a love that goes beyond deep emotion, relationship clichés, and romantic rhetoric. That's the kind of love I have witnessed through my parents—a selfless love that sows commitment against all odds, inconvenience, and even pain, and reaps action, not just hollow sentiment. It's a love that is as it does and is rooted in something greater than everything this world has to offer.

I find that what man considers love and what God considers love are radically different. Human love is limited and inadequate to meet the deeper needs of the human heart. We ache for love, but worldly love can't fill a soul. Only God's love can. Everything about God and His love reaches in from the eternal as He makes loving decisions that result in our highest good without compromising truth, reality, or what is right. His love is selfless and sacrificial—period! When we choose to walk in His love, it results in a desire to give what's most valuable: our time, talent, and treasure—even our very lives. Whenever you give away something of great value, something that's costly to give, there's pain involved. Love hurts. But the pain it costs is worth it because the joy in giving is always greater than the hurt.

To know the love I've been talking about, the love I have witnessed, you must know its source—*the One who is Love*. We cannot know love unless we know God. And we cannot know God unless we have been drawn to Him through His Son, Jesus, by the power and work of the Holy Spirit. It all goes back to God—as it should—since He is the Creator, Sustainer, and Giver of every good and perfect gift.

All of this has shown me that love looks like a mother I can risk telling anything to and trust to give honest, loving advice. A mother who pays any price for her children—including the son whose renowned silence echoes through countless hearts and speaks deeper than most words; a father making time to motivate me and help me be the best I can be, who could be as tender as he was tough and share a strong hug and a simple yet profound word or two of encouragement; a sister who's my best friend and so much more; and on it goes....

And although I have shared examples of what love has looked like in my life, the greatest act of love ever known is the perfect love of God displayed through His Son, Jesus, on the cross. (More about this is Appendix B.) We all have that same emptiness and longing to be filled, to be loved. However, nothing we strive after in this world can fill an empty soul. Not human love. Not toys or distractions. Not status. Not money or sex. Nothing. And that's reality. God alone is love, and in receiving Him and His gift of love the human heart is filled completely, as it was designed to be, with a love that overflows and touches everything around it. It is a love whose source is not of this world. And because this world doesn't give it to us, nothing in this world can take it away.

by faith...

We crave love. We want it so desperately that most of us spend ourselves in its pursuit, and in the end we find ourselves weary, restless, unsatisfied, and disillusioned. Why? Because the love we most desire is a gift. We don't have to go searching for it. All we need to do is receive it from the One who longs to give it to us. God's unconditional, selfless love is a gift. Nothing in this world can bring the meaning, joy, fullness, and hope our hearts crave. But God's gift of love can do all of that and more.

> How great is the love the Father has lavished upon us, that we should be called children of God! And that is what we are! —1 John 3:1

> This is how we know what love is: Jesus Christ laid down his life for us. And we ought to lay down our lives for our brothers. —1 John 3:16

> Dear friends, let us love one another, for love comes from God. Everyone who loves has been born of God and knows God. Whoever does not love does not know God, because God is love. This is how God showed his love among us: He sent his one and only Son into the world that we might live through him. This is love: not that we loved God, but that he loved us and sent his Son as an atoning sacrifice for our sins. Dear friends, since God so loves us, we also

ought to love one another. No one has ever seen God; but if we love one another, God lives in us and his love is made complete in us. —1 John 4:7–12

And so we know and rely on the love God has for us. God is love. —1 John 4:16

We love because he first loved us. —1 John 4:19

God's love for us cannot be measured. It is not only perfect in its effect, it is infinite in its extent. No calamity that may come upon us, however great it may be, can carry us beyond the pale of God's fatherly love for us. —Jerry Bridges[1]

---

1 Jerry Bridges, *Trusting God: Even When Life Hurts* (Colorado Springs, CO: NavPress, 1988, 2008), 153.

Chapter 5

○ ○ ○

FORGIVENESS AND THE HATERS

hope your dad dies."

My heart started racing, and the palms of my hands and my forehead began to perspire as I looked up from my cell phone in horror. I immediately felt like I was going to pass out. As I scrolled through my Twitter timeline, a notification popped up and so I checked it. That hate-filled message landed on both mine and Camryn's accounts at about the same time.

"Mom, look at this," I stammered as I handed her my phone.

Tears welled up in my eyes as I watched my mother read the evil tweet. She put her hand over her mouth in shock, and in eerie slow motion sat down on the hotel bed near where we were standing. Grammie walked into the room as Mommy began to cry. I handed her my phone so she could read the tweet as well.

"Oh my goodness," she said with a look of dread on her face. "I can't believe someone would say this. I can't believe it."

Grammie sat down next to my mom and hugged her. We were completely horrified—it was one of the cruelest things that had ever happened to us during some of the darkest days as my dad fought for his life. And although I was overwhelmed with emotion and pain, my heart ached for Camryn, who had received the same hateful message. She was only fourteen years old at the time, and I knew this was more than her heart could bear. All I wanted in that moment was to hold her, to tell her that everything was going to be okay. I longed to protect her from the cruelty and bitterness of the world. She's been through an immense amount of pain, and, as her big sister, I feel it is my duty to protect her at all cost.

On March, 21, 2014 my parents, Uncle Danny, and my father's executive assistant and close friend of our family, Tricia, flew to Lenox Hill Hospital in New York City to seek help in managing the intense pain my dad was experiencing due to the cancer in his jaw. They were hoping it would be a quick visit, but it turned into a ton of tests, scans, medications, and eventually chemo and radiation treatments. What they thought would be pain management, surgery, and recovery, ended up being cancer that had spread to the point where surgery was no longer a viable treatment. It seemed like every time a doctor walked into my father's hospital room, more bad news was delivered. More and more doctors and specialists kept coming in, doing more tests, taking more blood, explaining more and more things we didn't understand, and eventually telling us more and more bad news. It was like being in a nightmare that you could not wake up from.

Everything at that time was awful. It seemed like nothing was going right and that everything that could go wrong, did. Staring down the barrel of that horrific, cruel message I felt like I'd been punched in the stomach, and my mom looked like she wanted to throw up. What happened next was even more shocking, at least by this world's standards. We were all staring at each other, discussing what would make someone say something so hateful.

Mommy wiped her tears, sniffed, and said, "This guy must be

so sad, angry, and empty. As crazy as it sounds and is, I feel sorry for him. And I think we need to pray for him right now."

Huddled together, we held hands and began to intercede for the Twitter stranger. I suppose we had every reason and could have easily justified retaliating by responding back to the tweet, fighting fire with fire. Initially, that's exactly what we all wanted to do, but instead we chose to forgive and do the most loving thing we could for him—pray and ask God to do what only He could do in his heart and ours. Afterward, we sat in silence for a few minutes, still stunned by all that had happened. Oddly, I felt an overwhelming peace and compassion fill my heart like I had never experienced before.

Talk about Kelly Tough. I felt so weak and violated by this Twitter bully that praying for him was the last thing I wanted to do and certainly one of the toughest things I ever had to do. Yet as I did, in my weakness I grew immeasurably stronger as forgiveness began to fill my heart, replacing anger and hatred.

While forgiving is an act, forgiveness is an attitude, a way of life. We all make mistakes and need mercy and grace on a daily basis. Nobody's perfect and we all have blind spots. Instead of looking for reasons to hate, look for reasons to forgive. Life hurts and, as we mentioned in the previous chapter, love hurts too. If you're going to be victorious, you have to take the risk and learn to fight through the pain. I've learned that one of the best ways to do this is to walk in forgiveness—which really is an expression of love. One can't be separated from the other. Both must coexist, because you can't love without being willing to forgive.

Forgiving that Twitter guy allowed me to experience compassion in a way that I had never experienced it before. In walking it out and forgiving him, I was able to cultivate an attitude that eventually helped me heal, a forgiving attitude that also countered any

If you're going to be victorious, you have to take the risk and learn to fight through the pain. I've learned that one of the best ways to do this is to walk in forgiveness.

bitterness that very easily could have taken root in my heart, sending poison into the other relationships I treasured most. And let me tell you, this guy was extreme, but certainly not the only one who lashed out at us without cause. The cynicism and cold-heartedness that we had to confront during my dad's cancer battle was shocking at times.

My parents have tried to shield me from the hatred that seems to be part of the package when a member of your family is a public figure. Certainly, I didn't grow up in a bubble and have experienced what it's like to live in a world that's lost, hurting, and desperate for hope. I'm not immune to the fact that evil exists and runs rampant throughout the world.

Don't get me wrong: once my father's reoccurrence of cancer became public, it also sparked an unprecedented outpouring of love, prayer, and concern for our family like I have never witnessed before. The compassion and support that came to us knew no borders, cultural boundaries, or religious barriers as people reached out to us from literally across the globe. Unbelievably, nations such as Afghanistan, Ireland, and Germany found everyday people praying for us for a vast array of reasons. Sometimes it was simply because they were Buffalo Bills fans. And in some cases they didn't care for the Bills at all, but were Jim Kelly fans, wanting to support #12 as he battled against his greatest foe yet. In other cases, we heard from NFL fans who simply wanted to express their heartfelt concern about an NFL legend, while some had endured similar situations or had suffered the loss of a loved one to cancer.

I can't begin to tell you how all of these moving responses touched us. Or how these poignant expressions of goodwill overwhelmed, humbled, and blessed us beyond measure.

So why do I share all of this?

I guess because the hurt I have suffered at the hands of those my family or I have never wronged has taught me some valuable life lessons.

Haters are going to hate, but love always wins. We're not responsible for people's hatred and can't let their poison become ours. Like forgiveness, love is a way of life, a commitment to a person's highest good, independent of anything you may get out of it. That being said, you can't help but win in life if you're giving with no strings attached. Whether haters hate or lovers love, when you're committed to loving independent of what anyone else does, the scoreboard in the game of life always ends up in your favor.

We live in a world that is deeply wounded and hurting. And even though my years are not many, I have already learned that life generally does not go as we hope or plan. Death and pain, struggle and sorrow are experienced by all. Life plays no favorites. So in the end, what people will remember is the kind of person you were through the fiery trials. Whether the pressure compromised your love and integrity, or whether you remained true to what you knew was true.

My ability to stand against that pressure, and to forgive and love, was sorely tested by the last person on earth I'd ever have thought would hurt me—my father.

* * *

All I could think that night was that I felt a lot older than I did that morning. And though I'd been through my fair share, I didn't consider myself practiced at the art of life enough to be adequately equipped, offer advice, or speak with the wisdom of experience. That was all yet to come, and still is—I was just hitting my stride as a teenager, midway through high school. However, on the other side of a very unexpected and life-defining moment—a moment that taught me like no other—I found myself tested and proved genuine.

My mom and dad had this big brown couch in their bedroom that I would often do my homework on. So there I was one late afternoon, after school, just me and my math, when Daddy walked in. One thing I love about my dad is that what you see is what you get—and what I saw made me know I was going to get something off the beaten path. There was a tenderness and humility about him that was punctuated by an intense apprehension that I had never seen in him before.

"Erin, can I talk to you for a minute?" he asked haltingly.

I was suddenly on high alert, an anxious mixture of curiosity, uneasiness, and sheer wonder at what was coming next. "Sure, Daddy. What's up?"

With a huge sigh, the story tumbled out. He had been unfaithful to my mother. With tears in his eyes and sorrow in his voice, he explained how he had made choices that were not conducive to a healthy, unadulterated marriage. He asked me to forgive him for not being the best husband and father that he should have been and for hurting Mommy the way he did. He made no excuses—he really manned up. But as stunned and saddened as I was, I knew the temptations at the top of the NFL had gotten to him and he had caved. He wasn't the first superstar to do it, and wouldn't be the last, but he was *my father*, not the lurid headline in some scandal magazine.

Still, right then, all I could think about were the tears gathering in his eyes. And as hurt and angry as I was, I could see a man who was broken and so sincerely sorry that my heart quickly began to melt. Somewhat speechless, incredibly disappointed, and deeply wounded, I was able to search through his misty eyes and firmly say, "I forgive you, Daddy," as he pointedly and very humbly, I might add, asked it of me.

My thoughts then turned to my mom and what she must have

felt—Daddy said he had asked her forgiveness first. Still, her heart must be broken. She was drop-dead gorgeous and had to have had opportunities with equally gorgeous guys that she resolutely declined. Daddy had not; he blew it. He fumbled the ball and was trying to recover it and somehow turn it into a gain.

As I mentioned in an earlier chapter, I have heard my mother share her testimony of faith on numerous occasions. The part of her story that seems to resonate the most with women is her journey through my father's infidelity. At the end of her speaking engagements, she usually allows for a time of questions and answers from the audience. One of the first questions usually asked is something like this: "How in the world did you forgive Jim after all that he did to you?" Silence fills the room as my mother inhales and then shares her heart in the most vulnerable and beautiful way.

She says, "When God began to reveal to me how much He had forgiven me, it allowed room in my heart to fill up on His forgiveness so that that same forgiveness could flow out of my life into the lives of others. We can't receive the forgiveness of God and not extend it to others. In fact, in receiving God's love and forgiveness, a direct result of this should be that the same pours out of our lives. It's all God. You can't forgive or be forgiven without Him." (By the way, my mom is kind of deep, so oftentimes I need to write down what she says.)

The crazy thing is, she goes on to share how God has not only helped her to forgive but also to forget. Yes, I said *forget*. Of course it's not as if God supernaturally erased my mother's memory of what my father did to her, even though He can do that, but rather it's the forgetting of the pain it caused. As crazy as it sounds (and trust me, I know this all might sound a bit crazy) my mother will tell you that she has forgotten the pain. It doesn't hurt anymore.

Love always wins.
We're not responsible
for people's hatred
and can't let their
poison become ours.
Like forgiveness,
love is a way of life,
a commitment to
a person's highest
good, independent
of anything you
may get out of it.

Why? Because in truly forgiving God also works in us the ability to forget.

Honestly, now that I think about it, my dad didn't have to tell me what happened. He didn't have to ask me to forgive him. What had happened was between the two of them, and they could have worked it out privately. Yet my father felt that I deserved to know, and not just know what he did but know him—all of him—the good, the bad, and the ugly. And more amazingly, he felt that somehow his unfaithfulness to my mother had hurt me too—and he was right. I was devastated. How do you come to grips with your father's humanness in such shattering circumstances? Yet, I couldn't deny that there was something so real and honorable about the risk he ran sharing his moral failure with me, that even though I needed a good cry and then some, I *wanted* him to come out victorious, even better than he was before it all happened.

The sorrow and sense of loss that swept over me were smothering. Even though I had said the words, "I forgive you," to my dad after he had told me, and thought I meant what I said—living it out was and is something altogether different. But I realized that as much as it hurt, I *wanted* to forgive him. I had to make the choice to forgive and embrace my father in all his humanity, honesty, and love. At a certain point along the way to healing, I looked at my hands and saw that they weren't reaching out, they were instead withholding the very forgiveness that God had so freely given to me—forgiveness He gave so I would freely extend it to others. And once I did, I couldn't help but take a step closer, admiring my dad all the more in a very different but deeper and probably more mature way.

Maybe I've never fallen as far as my dad has, but sin is sin no matter how small or great. In the grand scheme of sin's deadliness, does it really matter if you fall five hundred or five thousand feet? Both landings have the same result. And even though my words fall far short of capturing the hurt, my decision in that crucial moment (which in all honesty took time to fully walk out) truly defined me as a daughter, and as a person. For in choosing to embrace my responsibility to love and forgive when I had the right to do the opposite, I not only grew closer to my father, but to God as well.

While I'm sure it wasn't God's first choice, He used my dad's infidelity to help him realize that his sin was tougher than he was—this realization and the death of my brother, Hunter, led my dad to reach out to Jesus and surrender his life to Him. It still amazes me that in his utter helplessness, weakness, and sorrow, he found the strength to rise above it all. And so did I. With my father, it was the strength to humble himself, confess what he had done, and receive God's forgiveness and love. With me, it was the strength to be Kelly Tough, forgive, and unconditionally love the one man in the world I longed to love more than any other—my dad.

Honestly, I am just flat out not schooled enough in this thing we call "life" to carry this conversation much further—I have too many bends to go around yet, more mistakes to make and living to do. However, I can tell you this: that since my father's confession and the Twitter man's vicious slur, I have been able to see myself more clearly, and by God's amazing grace I continue to press on one day at a time, one hurt at a time, one act of forgiveness at a time.

by faith...

Because of the limitless grace, mercy, and forgiveness God has extended to us, we have everything we need to offer forgiveness, grace, and mercy to anyone who has hurt or wronged us. This includes the people whom we would never dream would hurt us, as well as those who have shown great contempt and hatred unjustly. This is impossible in our own strength, but through God's indwelling Spirit, all things are possible.

> Bear with each other and forgive whatever griev-
> ances you may have against each other. Forgive as
> the Lord forgave you. And over all these virtues put
> on love, which binds them all together in perfect
> unity. —Colossians 3:13–14

Chapter 6

∘ ∘ ∘

JACK DANIELS, SAINT ANNE'S BONE, AND JESUS

There's probably more Jack Daniels in Uncle Ray than Jesus, or so you might assume.

To watch him from a distance for any length of time you would more than likely conclude that Ray Kelly, the third brother of the six Kelly boys, is the life of the party. And he is. If you're around Uncle Ray and you're human, you'll end up laughing, sometimes to the point of tears! So what happens when the life of the party—the one you don't leave home without if you want to have a good time—what happens when he prays?

We had only been in New York City a few days, and my father was not doing well at all. He was dehydrated, in excruciating pain, and growing weaker by the hour. We were all a wreck and felt helpless just watching and waiting as the doctors tried to manage the pain and determine the next steps in Daddy's cancer treatment process. It was late in the evening and time for us to head back to the hotel so that Daddy could try to sleep. Before leaving the hospital, we gathered around his bed to pray. As we held hands, Mom looked over at Uncle Ray and said, "Why don't you pray this time, Ray?"

He hesitated and stammered, "Oh well, I don't know about that." Daddy came to his brother's rescue, wisely interjecting, "Just say what's in your heart." Uncle Ray took the handoff and began to pray. "There are some mean things in my heart, God. Mean things. But please, heal my brother. I would take his place in a heartbeat if I could." And that was it. After Ray prayed, we all took turns hugging my dad good-bye and filed out of the room so he could get some rest.

Uncle Ray offered a modest and unassuming prayer. It was to the point, nothing especially spiritual. Nor was it delivered in "Christianese." (My dad often uses this word, which basically describes the language common to the Christian community that most people don't understand.) In fact, Daddy has often said that he doesn't speak Christianese because he doesn't talk like Mommy does. Uncle Ray was definitely not fluent in Christianese, or anything Jesus, so he simply spoke from his heart.

Despite the simplicity of his prayer, it was radical and honest and everything I wanted to be in that moment. I had mean things in my heart too, things I would never say out loud unless I was alone so no one could hear. He had more guts than me. I struggled with thoughts, feelings, emotions, and words that are better left unsaid or screamed into a pillow, things I'd be ashamed to admit but know that God hears, sees, and is aware of—yet somehow He loves me anyway.

Oddly, it was as if the sorrow that poured from my heart and through my eyes spoke louder and more sincerely than any words ever could. And still, the words were there buried deep, longing to claw their way out of my grave-like heart (surely they were words that brought death and not life), struggling to find their escape.

I walked away from that prayer and my father's bedside convicted and challenged. I couldn't wait to get back to the hotel so I could get alone with God. My mind and heart were flooded with questions. *What mean things do I have in my heart? If I could, would I take my father's place? Am I that honest and unguarded before God?* As soon as I could, I began frantically journaling and pouring out my heart to the Lord.

> *Lord, I don't know if I would take Daddy's place. And if I don't know, I suppose that means I wouldn't. But Uncle Ray would. I'm supposed to be living the "less of me and more of You" life and in an instant, in the midst of a simple prayer, I come face-to-face with the reality that I'm not as selfless as I would hope to be. Lord, forgive me! Please help me to be more like You. Help me to be completely vulnerable, open, and honest with You in every way. Like Uncle Ray, search my heart—all the mean and ugly that's there. Please expose it all, Lord, and lead me to a place of sweet grace and repentance. I am so sorry. Thank You for loving me. Thank You for revealing truth to me so that I can be set free to be fully me—no matter what. Please heal Daddy.*

I'll never forget Uncle Ray's prayer and my time with God that night; the honesty, sincerity, and vulnerability wrecked and humbled me. A man who never prayed taught me the most important aspect of intimacy with God: authenticity—just being real. And as a result of being real with God, I experienced a freedom like never before. Freedom to come to God just as I am with all of me—my mean things, questions, doubts, fears, hurts, anger, and tears. And I was also able to experience a fresh wave of gratitude as I recognized in the midst of my mess that I don't have to have it all together! God meets me right where I am. He's not going to fall off the throne in shocked disbelief if I honestly bring my "mean things" to Him. The fact is that if I had to have it all together in order to approach Him, I would never come—no one would. Our mess is the very place where Jesus comes to the rescue in order to take all of our brokenness and make it into something absolutely beautiful.

Uncle Ray was with us for extended periods of time during the months my dad battled cancer. We became accustomed to him being around, and when he decided to go home, we were sad, and he left with tears in his eyes. This man—the one I've always seen as the crazy uncle, a man with mean things in his heart—showed me one of the most beautiful things about freedom, love, and authentic prayer. And he really would've taken my father's place if he could—without hesitation. The sincerity with which Uncle Ray was willing to bear his brother's burden was both profound and convicting—and it changed my life.

Similarly, we have had many prayer experiences, each challenging and changing us in their own unique way. Among the more unusual was the day my parents were entreated to kiss Saint Anne's bone. Yep, you read right. In an effort to heal my father of cancer, they were invited to kiss a piece of bone said to have been a part of the body of Saint Anne, the mother of the Virgin Mary—Jesus' grandma.

While I was away at college, our dear family friend Dennis brought a nun over to pray for Daddy. She was soft-spoken, gentle, yet formidable and a force to be reckoned with for sure. She was invited to our home because we were desperate for healing and prayer for my dad, and she was ready to bring her "A game" with God right into our living room. This sweet sister (I apologize and mean no disrespect by not sharing her name) brought a somewhat

Our mess is the very place where Jesus comes to the rescue in order to take all of our brokenness and make it into something absolutely beautiful.

intriguing relic with her that was supposedly used for healing the sick. She cradled the tiny treasure in her hand while explaining how it would be used; it was a piece of Saint Anne's bone—literally. Saint Anne, she said, was the Virgin Mary's mother. The sister went on to share that her own mother had given the precious relic to her before she died. It was held in a flower-shaped locket because it was smaller than a mustard seed, and you could see through the glass encasement that held the tiny nugget of bone.

The nun took charge, explaining that she was going to pray, and that after she prayed she would give everyone an opportunity to kiss the small encasement that held the piece of bone. My parents were confused and taken aback. *Kiss the bone,* my mom thought to herself. *Umm, I don't think so.* She began silently praying as her heart and mind wrestled while the soft-spoken but determined nun went on and on about the ancient artifact. "God, I can't kiss that bone," my mother whispered. *Jim's healing doesn't rest upon us kissing an ancient woman's bone fragment,* she thought to herself. *And how in the world can that actually be Mary's mother's bone? And even if it is, can it take away cancer? Really?*

As my mother questioned in silence, the nun started to pray. Her words were beautiful, and my mom said she couldn't help but be in complete agreement with everything the nun was praying. But, the struggle over kissing the bone was still fiercely surging through my mother's soul with no resolution in sight. She was still talking to God about it. And to her amazement, in the midst of the praying and the wrestling, God gave her an overwhelming peace. She explained to me that she understood what the Lord was trying to tell her about the nun and the bone. It wasn't about the bone at all; it wasn't about the nun or what she prayed either. It was about God and what He was going to do in all of our hearts. The nun came to our home with sincere and pure motives, to do what she could to help my dad. This was all that she knew to do—so she did it. In the midst of all that was going on, my mother said she heard the words, "It's okay." Suddenly, as if to confirm what her heart was speaking, she was reminded of the words in 1 Samuel 16:7: "The LORD does not look at the things people look at. People look at the outward appearance, but the Lord looks at the heart." The LORD looks at the heart. Outwardly the bone thing seemed very bizarre, but the nun truly wanted to see God glorified through healing Daddy—and that motivation was enough.

The group continued to pray and then the nun put the relic up to my mother's mouth so she could kiss it—literally. My mom was the first one the nun approached. Her eyes were closed, but she could feel the nun's hands that held the little bone less than an inch from her mouth. *What am I going to do? I heard what God said—"It's okay."* Furiously, she pondered. But in that moment, she just wasn't completely sure what that meant. *It's okay to kiss the bone?* She didn't have time to think about it anymore, so she reached her hand up and grabbed the two fingers that held Saint Anne's small bone and clutched the relic. But....

Try as she might, my mom couldn't bring herself to kiss it, so instead, she kissed her own thumb, the one holding the relic. It happened in a split second. Mommy didn't want to offend the nun, but she just couldn't bring herself to actually kiss the bone—and so, she kissed her own thumb. Can we just pause right now and take in the fact that God has a sense of humor?

As the nun moved on to Daddy, who was sitting next to my mom, she couldn't help but wonder if the nun caught her act—if she was busted. The thing is, God knew and she was sorting it out with Him even as the whole thing unfolded. In the meantime, she didn't dare open her eyes but could hear Daddy, Uncle Ray, and our friend Dennis as they all kissed the bone.

As the nun continued the unorthodox ritual, my mom found herself frozen in the moment, somewhat confused, and yet at peace. It was weird and unusual, but then again, so was Jesus. And she had peace in the midst of her unanswered questions because she knew that God was at work in the midst of it all. She understood that there was no power in the bone and no kiss that can cure cancer. If there's any linkage at all, it's that kissing the relic is an expression of faith in God—and that faith would unleash a power greater than the battle my dad was in.

God was at work that day. He knew exactly what had motivated the nun to come by for a visit, to pray over Daddy, and to have my parents kiss the bone. God sees our hearts and He knows, and that's why *it's okay*. Once again, we know it's okay because He knows. And if He knows, that's enough. We don't need to understand; we just need to trust and rest in Him.

We have all had our lives transformed in the most unexpected ways, and though we have been around many corners through this trial, there seems to always be a new turn of events that catches us off guard. One of the more resounding, soul-shaking prayer experiences we had was with a man we encountered in the hospital.

His name was Jason. He was in his late thirties, and when we met him, he had just weeks to live. Cancer may have ravaged his body, but a jubilant hope flourished in his heart. We had the privilege of meeting him as we were anxiously packing up Daddy's hospital room to head out to yet another scan. Cataloging a litany of appointment dates and times, scans, blood work, diagnostic tests, and clinical abbreviations, we "huddled up" in the hospital room, as is our custom, to call the next play and plan the next move.

Jason graciously entered our world after my father had endured a very difficult night, and was having trouble keeping food and water down due to some pain medication. And as the nurse reviewed his final release instructions, he graciously interrupted her. "Wait a minute. I want to give away the flowers." Every time he leaves the hospital, he gives another patient the flowers that have been sent to him so they can enjoy them too. I'm surprised he remembered the flower-give-away routine because he was completely drained and felt so sick.

"I know the perfect person," the astonished nurse replied. And so, with flowers in hand instead of a football, #12 was wheeled down the hall and around the corner into Jason's room. This complete stranger who was to dominate our conversation for days to come looked up in sheer disbelief, ecstatic to see Jim Kelly in his room. It was obvious that the nurses and everyone else in the room couldn't help but feed off of the contagious joy radiating from this man. You would never have known he had just weeks to live. Jason celebrated every heartbeat and acted more alive while he was dying than most people who enjoy perfect health.

After a short visit, we took a few photos and said our goodbyes. But as Daddy climbed back into his wheelchair, before we could head out the door, we were interrupted as Jason asked, "Jim, can I pray for you?" A beautiful, overwhelming silence wrapped itself around us, followed by one of the most precious and moving prayers I have ever experienced. I wish I could remember everything Jason said to God. I wish I could adequately explain what it was like to have a young man dying of cancer, given just weeks to live—a mere handful of heartbeats—pray for my father, the man who was fighting for his life because of the same dreadful disease that was taking Jason's.

As soon as Jason stopped praying, Daddy looked up at him, moved by compassion, laid his hand on Jason's shoulder, and began to pray. And after he stopped praying, we all just stood there, overwhelmed.

As we left Jason's room and made our way to the elevator, his joy went with us. Little was said because we could feel the hope he shared from the depths of his soul take root in the depths of ours—words would've fallen so short.

And in a way they still do.

Jason radiated such joy and lived in the light of eternity so extremely that the soft glow and promise of the world to come cast its warmth across our souls. He gave us a glimpse of what it's like to suffer well, praise Him in the storm, and walk courageously by faith and not by sight. It gave a whole new meaning to "Kelly Tough." But there's even more to this incredible story....

Not long after, we invited our pastor over to pray with Daddy. The house was starting to fill up as the Kelly brothers made their way over one by one, along with friends and teammates. After some small talk and an update on everything that had transpired over the last few weeks, we were ready to pray when the doorbell interrupted us. My mother jumped up to get it and found Peter John, a long-time close friend, at the door. We exchanged greetings, made the necessary introductions, and then prepared to go back to prayer.

Before Pastor Jerry began, however, he said, "Before we pray, I'd like to tell you something that I think will encourage you," upon which he recounted how before he came to our house he had had a meeting with another pastor in the area. During that meeting, the other pastor shared with Jerry how he had visited a young man, a member of his church, in the hospital the day before. Jerry went on to explain how this young man was in his late thirties and dying of cancer.

As Pastor Jerry continued to share the story his pastor friend had recounted, I knew it was Jason. And it was. If you know me at all, this is the point when I start freaking out, ready to jump out of my skin. I could hardly contain the joy! And it gets even better.

Amazingly, as Pastor Jerry was talking, not only did we realize that his friend was Jason's pastor, but Daddy interrupted mid-sentence and said, "Wait a minute, Peter John, before we left the hospital we gave Jason the flowers you sent us." To which Peter John responded with a look of awe on his face: "You've got to be kidding me."

I couldn't help but think of Romans 8:28: "And we know that in all things God works for the good of those who love him, who have been called according to his purpose." You can trace the hand of God weaving these destinies together to craft a beautiful tapestry of His glory throughout this incredible story—those few miraculous moments in time where His love and compassion were tangible, felt by those who were there and now can be shared by all who hear this remarkable story.

Through the joy of a dying man, another warrior fighting the battle is given hope, and is blessed beyond measure. And while we can't understand the many challenging circumstances that our destinies are fashioned from, it does inspire us to pray that God's will *will* be done. For in the midst of suffering, we find a contagious joy and shared hope that causes both men to not just endure this trial but to triumph through it.

It is no easy task to find strength in weakness, hope in the midst of despair, or life, joy, and faith in spite of suffering. It's not easy, but it's there for the finding—Jason found it. As the oldest daughter of an NFL legend whom I've really only known as "Daddy," my heartache watching him battle this demon, bigger and meaner than any he met on the field—cancer—brought tears that fell from a place deeper than I've ever known.

Kelly Tough could well be an expression of how God uses

Kelly Tough could well be an expression of how God uses what the enemy means for evil to strengthen a family for good.

what the enemy means for evil to strengthen a family for good. My sorrow and the resulting pressure have driven me to my knees and radically changed my relationship with both my earthly father and heavenly Father—which, in turn, has radically changed me. You see, the hurt has led to a hope, deep and enduring through my faith in Jesus Christ—who is bigger than any and every battle we face. Trust me when I tell you that it is these heart-wrenching experiences looming far beyond my power to withstand that have taught me what true strength is.

While survival and sacrifice have tested us, staining the pages of our story with many tears, God's boundless grace, love, forgiveness, and hope are woven throughout it in a way that holds it all together. And if there's an object lesson to being Kelly Tough, that's it—His ability in our inability, His strength in our weakness, our standing against any and all odds when we kneel before Him.

Prayer is powerful. I've seen the impact firsthand and I'm continually amazed. What amazes and humbles me the most is the fact that God already knows all things. He knows every single word that will come rolling off of our tongues before we pray anything. He knows the requests we keep silent, our thoughts, intentions, and motives. He sees us, all of us—what we can see in the mirror's reflection and what we hide. And yet, He beckons us, invites us to come to Him anyway. That being said, this should motivate us to be sincere, open, and honest, pouring our hearts out before the God who sees us and knows.

Another thing about prayer that blows me away is the fact that some of the greatest blessings in our lives end up being the result of prayers that have been answered in a completely different way than we would ever have expected. God always answers prayer, but not always in the way we desire.

There's a quote by Oswald Chambers that is tacked to the office wall behind our desktop computer. It reads, "Let us never forget that our prayers are heard, not because we are in earnest, not because we suffer, but because Jesus suffered." I can't tell you how many times I've read this quote. Oddly, its significance grabbed hold of my heart only recently. Prayer is a gift, but the greater gift is the One to whom we pray, the One who made prayer possible—the One who longs to have a relationship with us and laid down His life in order to make sure He could.

Lastly, and this is going to sound a bit crazy, what we often seek through prayer is an end result, an answer—and rightfully so, sort of. We want a certain outcome. For example, when I was praying for my dad, I wanted God to heal him. But what I didn't realize and what I am still learning is that God wants us to have more of Himself rather than the answer to our prayers—because He is the answer. Sometimes He will withhold what we think we want in order to give us what we actually need—more of Him.

And so, my prayer life has changed drastically, and continues to do so. Yes, I still pray and talk to God and ask Him for specific outcomes—I talk to Him about everything. But now, it's really more about getting to know Him rather than getting what I want. Oddly, I've learned that the more of Him He reveals to me, the more I long for and the more my prayer life continues to grow and change, the more my relationship with God deepens—and that is far greater than answered prayer.

by faith...

I don't think God likes speaking Christianese, though He's reluctantly fluent in it. Instead, I think He loves the language of the heart and loves people who are real. Because of this, He can hear and respond to anyone's prayers. We never have to fake it with God. From the intellectual and the pastor able to quote books of the Bible, to the humble homemaker serving her family, if we speak from our heart, God hears and moves to bring all things together for our good and His amazing glory.

> Be joyful always; pray continually; give thanks in all circumstances, for this is God's will for you in Christ Jesus. —1 Thessalonians 5:16–18

> Let us never forget that our prayers are heard, not because we are in earnest, not because we suffer, but because Jesus suffered.
> —Oswald Chambers[1]

---

[1] Oswald Chambers, *If You Will Ask: Reflections on the Power of Prayer* (Grand Rapids, MI: Discovery House Publishers, 1937, 1989).

Chapter 7

○ ○ ○

GREATNESS BEYOND THE GRIDIRON

I f I could switch his head with mine, I would."

Hall of Fame running back, and my dad's best friend and former teammate, Thurman Thomas told the *CBS This Morning* reporter those words. The actual conversation between my dad and Thurman went something like this.

Daddy said, "You just don't know how bad my head is feeling right now."

"If I could take your head for a little bit," Thurman said, "for a little while, I would switch it with mine. I know how tough an individual you are and to see you struggling and going through the pain that you're going through. I'm here for you."

So what do I mean when I talk about greatness beyond the gridiron? Well, what I'm referring to are the countless NFLers who jumped into my dad's world and dropped anchor through the toughest days of his cancer treatment. There were a lot of guys who played alongside him on the field and who stayed alongside him in the hospital, and a few who played against him too. They were like angels to us, who, in their own way, joined the battle against this monstrous enemy by offering love, companionship, encouragement, support, and all kinds of laughter.

Former teammates Thurman Thomas, Andre Reed, and Bruce Smith went from helping raise the Bills' score back when they all played together to raising my dad's spirits when they came by the house to give him a sendoff as he left for New York City. He was gearing up for a six-week tour that was to include surgery, pain management, chemotherapy, and radiation and it turned out to be very demoralizing. And yet in the throes of a very challenging time, even for one of the NFL's toughest quarterbacks, all three of them also made the trip to visit him.

Actually, Thurman and my father passed the time while in the hospital by putting together puzzles that were anonymously sent by a fan. This particular one was a picture of an elephant, and the welcome distraction wound up becoming an Internet sensation, leading fans from all over to deluge my dad with puzzles everyone worked on when they came to visit him. I'm pretty sure he is set for life in the jigsaw puzzle department. Of course, you've got to have a competitive spirit to win in the NFL, so naturally, when Bruce Smith visited, he wanted to do a bigger and better puzzle with my dad than he and Thurman had assembled.

These guys were as tender as they were tough, and as steadfast as they were strong. And while Thurman, Bruce, and Andre were part of the hometown team, the visiting squad was fantastic as well. Boomer Esiason, who had a fourteen-year career as a quarterback in the NFL, visited him in New York City, and the record-breaking Dan Marino, who was drafted the same year as my father, surprised him in the Big Apple and in Buffalo. Once Dan came armed with fresh stone crabs from Miami. Additionally, sportscaster Chris Berman, former teammate Steve Tasker, Bills' wide receiver Sammy Watkins, Bill Polian, and many others dropped in to offer my dad encouragement in the midst of his journey. And on top of all those greats, my dad's former coach, Hall of Famer Marv Levy, called almost daily and came by when he returned to Buffalo for a visit.

It was a beautiful sight to see the team (more like our extended family really) rally behind my father, and it meant so much to all of us. But of all the people who rallied behind him and had my dad's back, no one had it like the guy who had it on game day, his friend and former backup quarterback, #14, Frank Reich. Back in the day when they played together, Frank had to know everything my dad knew and be ready to step into the game at a moment's notice. And if you remember, while he was doing just that, he led the Bills to the greatest comeback win in NFL history against the Houston Oilers in 1993.

Being a backup quarterback demands a servant's heart. You work as hard as the starting QB but receive none of the glory or accolades—you're a leader-in-waiting while the limelight belongs to another. To be as good at it as Frank was requires exemplary character, a healthy sense of self-confidence, and a passionate commitment to both the team you're on and the guy who has the job you would love to have. That was and is Frank Reich—he's the epitome of "greatness beyond the gridiron," plus so much more. And just as he stepped in when my dad wasn't able to take another snap on the field, once again, though off the field this time, Frank stepped in for "Team Kelly" and for God's team to encourage his friend and brother in Christ.

Galatians 6:2 tells us to "carry each other's burdens, and in this way you will fulfill the law of Christ." Well, Frank told my father that since he couldn't be there for him physically, he was going to send him a text message every day of his radiation and chemo treatments. And he did just that. He never missed a day and delivered

Aren't we all called to be His arms that reach to the hurting, be His voice that speaks life and encouragement to the dying and downtrodden, be His hope to those whose false hopes have left them hopeless?

some forty-plus of the most inspirational text messages we've ever read.

One of earlier messages, sent at the beginning of the second week of the radiation treatments, read:

> Stand strong Chilly,[1] just like when you played.… You are still the leader and you still have a great supporting cast around you. Even though the weight of this battle is on your shoulders—you are the one with the ball standing in the pocket with blitzers coming from all angles—you are not fighting this battle alone.… You have family and friends who will do whatever possible—take confidence and courage in that!

He followed that up with selected verses from Psalm 31 that were extremely relevant to what my dad was going through at that particular time. Some of them that stuck out to my dad were verses such as Psalm 31:14–15:

> But I trust in you, LORD;
> I say, "You are my God."
> My times are in your hands;…

Because Frank realized that my dad wouldn't have his phone with him, and because the impact of the radiation treatment would preclude him from reading his texts some days, he copied my mom on every text he sent. At first she would only read them to my father when they came, but eventually, because they were so powerful, encouraging, and inspirational, she ended up sharing them with friends, family, and visitors—whomever happened to

---

[1] Chilly Factor 12 was his nickname for my dad.

be in the room. So ultimately, it wasn't just my mom and dad who were heartened by Frank's messages; everyone who heard them was challenged and changed for the better.

On the second day of the third week of chemo treatments, he sent this text message that brought back many memories to all who read it, as well as much encouragement to keep trusting in the Lord no matter what life brought to him—God is faithful:

> To this day I still tell people two stories about passes I have seen you throw. The first was when you threw a slant to your left—nothing hard about that, right? Except you did it on three steps rolling out to the left and hit Chris Burkett in perfect stride—no one else can make that throw. The second, was at the end of a half, you threw a Hail Mary to Andre (he was running down our sideline to your left side) you hit him in perfect stride—seventy-six yards in the air (I ran the tape back ten times just to make exactly sure). And here is the thing—it was into the wind! Andre was so shocked because the ball was in the air so long it ended up going through his hands. Crazy, crazy, crazy, nobody can make that throw! You had an absolute rocket for an arm.

Not too often, but every now and then, you witness a guy do something on the football field that is incredible—that few if any can do. I am thankful that I got to see you make those throws and a few more up close and in person. You made throwing the football look so easy—effortless—like you could throw it as far as you had to and as accurate as needed.

Well Jim, as amazing as that all sounds, here is something a million times more amazing and is Good News for all who know and believe: The God of heaven and earth, the Lord Almighty,

Jesus is His name—guess what? He can move mountains! He can command the storm to stop and it listens, He parted the sea for His people, made water come from a rock, and fed His people in the desert for forty years. He can give sight to the blind and hearing to the deaf. He heals all kinds of diseases. And here is the thing: He makes it look easy—it's effortless to Him. Just search the Scriptures, over and over and over again we see the Lord has complete power over all the earth. Yes, we do understand that the Lord doesn't "fix" everything right now—but here is what gives us hope. He can fix it if it fits into His purposes and we also know that even if He doesn't fix it now…that ultimately all things will be made right upon His return. So that puts you/us in good hands—God is good and God is all-powerful!

This portion of a text that Frank sent at the onset of the fourth week of radiation was especially meaningful to me because it reflected my own understanding of what it means to be Kelly Tough as a follower of Christ:

Jim, your schedule this week is difficult—more difficult than any of us can imagine with the chemo treatment. It doesn't matter…expect to WIN! No matter how sick you get or how bad you feel, keep fighting to WIN. You can't do it alone—your family is there to support you…and remember, this is their battle as well. Lead them. Show them how to fight. Your girls were too young to see you fight as a player…but not now; show them what "Kelly Tough" is all about!

You don't have to be Superman; none of us are bulletproof. Just be you…and remember that in your weakest moments Christ's power is perfected in you.

He included Psalm 77:11–14 with that message, which was really encouraging to us since we were just past the midway point in the radiation therapy:

Our ultimate backup is Jesus who comes to the rescue and carries us through when the journey is too great. As He takes the field, He sends His warriors to help us fight through all that this life throws at us.

I will remember the deeds of the LORD;
yes, I will remember your wonders of old.
I will ponder all your work,
and meditate on your mighty deeds.
Your way, O God, is holy.
What god is great like our God?
You are the God who works wonders;
you have made known your might among the peoples.

And just two weeks later, he followed that message up with another one that explained what it meant to be Kelly Tough:

It is third and five—what are you gonna do…quick kick? I didn't think so…that is not in your DNA! Go ahead then and make the call…it's your choice—whether you huddle or make the call at the LOS (line of scrimmage), either way make the call with conviction and belief. Your teammates (most especially your family) are all here supporting and fighting with/for you. But you are still the leader and always will be! Now is not the time to back down, no matter the circumstances.

There is no shame in an incomplete pass or even having to punt every once in a while—you don't have to be the perfect leader and you don't have to do it all by yourself… but make no mistake, you still have to make the call for this day…how you approach this day will set the tone for the whole team much the same way you set the tone for our team every time we stepped on the field!

It got to the point that we began to really look forward to Frank's text messages, for they were like a daily devotional rooted in our reality that profoundly impacted us. Eventually, however, we got something even better than an inspiring text message; we got the inspiring man himself as he came to New York City to visit my dad in the hospital. It was a wonderful reunion where everyone spent time praying together, reminiscing, and catching up with the latest NFL news.

I learned a lot from the way Frank stepped right into his backup position again, not as a quarterback but as a Christian brother who really loved my dad and put legs on that love (so to speak). Just as that verse in Galatians 6:2 guides us to bear each other's burdens, Frank did all he could to strengthen my father's heart and keep pointing him to the source of his strength—the Lord. And isn't that what we are all called to do as Christians—as the body of Christ? Aren't we all called to be His arms that reach to the hurting, be His voice that speaks life and encouragement to the dying and downtrodden, be His hope to those whose false hopes have imploded and left them hopeless?

Our ultimate backup is Jesus who comes to our rescue and carries us through when our journey is too great. And as He takes the field, He sends His warriors to help us fight the good fight of faith in the midst of all that life throws at us.

Servant-leaders like Frank, Thurman, Bruce, Andre, and all the others who blessed my dad and us through this horrific battle are amazing and inspiring examples. They are emblematic of the faithfulness of God and the faithfulness of friends—the kind of people we're all called to be when someone is backed up against their own goal line and is trying to move the ball downfield against impossible odds. Their covenant loyalty reminds us that with God all things are possible, and with Him as our backup we'll always be victorious.

by faith...

We are not meant to do this life journey alone. We need God and we need each other. Every one of us will come against insurmountable circumstances and trials that will cause us to want to give up. However, God's plans for us are always good. In the midst of our trials His heart's desire is that we choose to seek Him as well as receive the counsel, comfort, and companionship of the people He has specifically placed in our lives for such a time as this. We are meant to carry one another's burdens—to be there for each other—to lighten the load. And when we do this, the amazing thing is we end up being blessed and receive way more than we give. We can never out-give God, but in being there for each other and giving of ourselves to those in our lives who need it most, we get to experience the blessing of His giving through ours.

> Carry each other's burdens, and in this way you will fulfill the law of Christ. —Galatians 6:2

> A friend loves at all times. —Proverbs 17:17

> Praise be to the God and Father of our Lord Jesus Christ, the Father of compassion and the God of all comfort, who comforts us in all our troubles, so that we can comfort those in any trouble with the comfort we ourselves have received from God.
> —2 Corinthians 1:3–4

Chapter 8

○ ○ ○

EVERY TEAR
TELLS A STORY

It's okay to cry!"
I could faintly make out his head hanging down through the
blinding tears that flooded my eyes. They streamed down my
face uncontrollably as the knot in my throat tightened until I could
barely breathe. I marshaled every last drop of willpower trying to
stifle my sobs as the toughest man I've ever known slowly lifted his
head, reluctantly yielding to the tears that forced their way from
his broken heart into his eyes.

And he began to cry.

It was inevitable, but that didn't make it any easier. In fact,
"easy" just wasn't in our vocabulary anymore. My dad had lost the
ability to eat by mouth as a result of the intense pain and numerous sores from radiation treatments. The doctor, as graciously as
possible, explained to my dad why he would need to have a feeding
tube put in. And though we all knew it was coming, it still made
us feel as if the ground gave way and we were desperately reaching
for arms to fall into as we braced for the inevitable impact. What
would be next? What else would he have to endure?

Seeing him cry only made me cry more—my big, tough father who was slammed to the turf by blitzing linebackers week after week, shaking off cuts, bruises, and concussions too numerous to count, only to rebound and put six points on the scoreboard. But there was no linebacker, and the numbers we were following were very different from the numbers on the scoreboard as he sat across from me with tears rolling down his cheeks. This wasn't football; it was life! Getting thrown for a loss in this forum meant losing a lot more than yardage. And that would explain why I had never seen tears like this before—tears filled with pain, frustration, confusion, and brokenness from one of the toughest guys on the planet!

As his little girl I was tough too. Tough but shattered—with my tears coming from a kind of heartbreak I had never felt before. Nearly paralyzed, all I could do was sit there and pray, hold his hand, and weep with him. And in that rare, recklessly vulnerable moment, we threw away the playbook, and allowed our unguarded eyes to meet, my father trusting me with his tears and me hanging my broken heart on my sleeve. I've never felt closer to my dad, never seen him stronger, and I don't think either of us have ever been more "Kelly Tough!"

There are only a few times that I recall seeing my dad cry. You see, when he grew up as one of six Kelly boys, intense wrestling matches (you might call them knock-down, drag-out) with his brothers usually led to someone getting hurt. Long before the gashes scabbed over, the typical response from my grandfather was, "Toughen up! You're a Kelly, and Kelly boys don't cry!"

It wasn't long before a similar sentiment was being echoed to the girls in our family. Seriously! When my aunt noticed my mom crying after Daddy took a fierce hit that sidelined him during one of the Super Bowl games, she quickly shot her the "eye" and bluntly snapped, "Kelly girls don't cry!"

Well, in the grand scheme of life, filled with the kind of circumstances we've walked through, Kelly girls and Kelly boys *do* cry. In fact, I'm convinced that this reflects strength of character and an enduring foundation for life—as opposed to pretending the hit doesn't hurt. It doesn't mean you don't play through the pain, but that you don't let the pain play you. There's freedom in being honest and calling it the way you see it!

This realization certainly didn't happen overnight. My dad is not one to wear his heart on his sleeve. He's the quarterback—the one calling the shots and holding the team together when everything's falling apart. Through most of my teenage years, I was a lot like him when it came to fielding my emotions. Sure, I had my moments, but most of the time I held my tears in, stuffing them until I couldn't take even one more emotional step beneath the weight of that proverbial "last straw."

The weight of my sorrow was relentless, and even the smallest demand felt like a boulder on my back. I was unable to unburden my heart, especially during the last few months, as I struggled watching my dad's recovery from his cancer treatments. But I'll be honest with you: it was a game changer. And with my dad's cancer, and everything that we've been through as a result, I have a whole new perspective on life, a whole new game plan, and I cry all the time now. Sometimes it's a few tears, other times they fall like rain, and I sob until my eyes are swollen shut and I can barely breathe. I've become convinced that tears are a gift, an expression of strength rather than weakness. I have learned to give myself permission to break free and cry. And that is exactly how I feel when I cry now—*free!*

In the midst of joy and sorrow, I have come to understand that every tear tells a story. Every time we weep it's linked to a feeling, a hurt, a laugh, a moment embroidered by God into the tapestry of our lives. And as I think back to the times I released the tears and allowed them to shape and mold me into who I am today, they represent some of those gathered moments, which, though painful and tear filled, have taught me what it means to be Kelly Tough—even when overwhelmed with deep sorrow and weakness.

I have discovered that there is a beautiful yet bewildering tension between joy and sorrow in this life. So rather than drain my energy in an unending struggle to grab hold of and cling to joy, I've decided to let joy and sorrow walk hand in hand. I began to understand how these two things could walk together while I was clinging to my father's arm, watching rainbow-colored balloons disappear in the distance. Let me explain.

It was Saturday afternoon, July 26, 2014. Staring down at the red helium balloon I held in my left hand, my right hand fiddled with a Sharpie marker as I pondered what to write. Hunter's favorite color was red, so this was the only balloon I wanted. Part of me delicately held onto it to keep it from flying away while another part of me desperately wanted to squeeze the balloon as hard as I could until it popped. Maybe this would help relieve the pain.

It would be impossible to write all I wanted to share with my brother on this small balloon. How I longed to tell him everything that had happened over the past year and all that God was doing in and through our family. I wanted to tell him about the battle Daddy had been in and how he had to have a feeding tube, oxygen, and even a suction machine in the hospital. I wanted to tell him how hard it was (and still is) to live in a world without Hunter James Kelly. With every joy and hurt anxiously trying to

I've become convinced that tears are a gift, an expression of strength rather than weakness.

escape my weary heart, I began to write, scribbling a short note that would soon fly away with the wind:

Hunter Boy,
Words can't describe how much I miss you.
I'm so proud to be your sister.
I can't wait to see you soon!
I love you, Hunter...SO MUCH!
Love, your big sister, Erin

It was short, simple, and to the point. I had so much more to say, but for some reason, my little note was enough—enough to bring a smile to my face and tears to my eyes. Hunter would understand.

We have been letting balloons go for as long as I can remember—a tradition with tremendous significance that will never end. Every year our Hunter's Hope families from all around the world come to Ellicottville, New York, to spend time with others who have a child with Krabbe and to learn more about this dreadful disease. We understand each other, and what it's like to love and care for someone with a terminal illness. Each of us knows the joy and pain of treasuring every breath, not knowing what the next day or even the next moment holds, but finding hope and peace in the One who holds it all together perfectly. And so every year we come together as one family, to celebrate life. On the last day we all gather to write messages on balloons and release them to heaven for the ones we love who are already there.

This day is hard—one of the hardest of the year. And yet it's also one of the best days. My family celebrates and rejoices in the life of Hunter—the boy who changed our lives in eight and a half brief years. We ache to be near him every single day; however, something about that day magnifies the hurt to a degree that is simply unexplainable. And yet at the same time, watching the balloons disappear into the blue sky brings an unexpected joy.

On that particular day, I clung to Daddy's arm, trying my best to follow the red balloon climbing through the heavens as every gathering tear made it harder to see. Soon it would vanish behind clouds and I would go about the rest of my day. Yet, in that moment, time stood still. All that seemed to exist were my tears and the red balloon in the sky. Camryn stood there and clung to my mom, as she always does when she's sad and misses her brother.

It wasn't long before Daddy had his arms around all of us. He wore sunglasses, but even those couldn't hide the pain in his eyes or the tears running down his cheeks. He misses his son. We all do. And until the day we see Hunter again, our pain and joy will continue to walk hand in hand.

That just seems to be the way of this world, a world that needs a Savior, a world that aches for love. And as I reflect on that day, I guess it explains why I'm standing here crying. Why is this so hard? My dad is still here. He's alive! Why allow fear, hurt, and anger to overcome what I know is true? God is bigger than cancer, and He holds my dad's life in His mighty hands!

* * *

I continued to wrestle with my heart and mind as I stood in the middle of Target trying my best to hold back tears. It was June 8, 2014, one week before Father's Day, and I was in the card aisle trying to decide which card would be perfect to give Daddy. After all he had been through and all he was still battling, it had to be the perfect card.

I looked through half the cards the store had to offer, but tears filled my eyes from the moment I opened the first one. It was short, to the point, and ended with "I love you." There was nothing extra special about this particular card or the meaning behind it. It was just an ordinary Father's Day card. But in my eyes, this was my dad's card, and something about that hit me harder than it ever had in the past.

I have celebrated this day nineteen times. From the moment I could scribble "Daddy" with a crayon on a sheet of paper, I have been making Father's Day cards; each one with a little note to let him know how much his little girl loves him. I remember trying my best to express just how great that love is and in doing so decided that this statement is the only one that truly gets the point across: "Daddy, I love you more than a million footballs!" I must say, in the Kelly house, that's a lot of love right there! And I'm pretty sure every one of my letters ended with "You're the best daddy in the world!"—something I still make sure to remind him of.

For the past nineteen years I have celebrated my dad twice a year: on Father's Day and his birthday, which is on Valentine's Day. Twice every 365 days. That means that I have celebrated my dad's life only thirty-eight times in the 6,935 days that I have lived on this earth. And truthfully, even thirty-eight is pushing it since I don't remember half of those from my early childhood years. Let's just say, when you're sitting in the hospital every day watching your dad suffer from cancer, your mind begins to run in a million directions. Not all of them good. *Why haven't I rejoiced in his life every single day? Why haven't I told him I loved him more? Why haven't I thanked God every day for choosing this man to be my dad?* Not only do you start asking all sorts of questions, but you think a lot and remember, fear, worry, laugh, cry, and experience every other emotion under the sun. Other times you just want to scream into a pillow or run into the woods by yourself

I don't know what
tomorrow holds, but
in this moment
I choose to trust
the God who
holds tomorrow.

and smash some plates. Okay, maybe that last thing is just me.

However, in the midst of all these emotions I have an entirely new perspective of what Father's Day is all about. I have never been so thankful to call Jim Kelly my dad, and I have never been so proud to be called his daughter. Not because he is one of the all-time best quarterbacks who took the Bills to four straight Super Bowls, but rather because he's the one who would do anything for me; the one who protects me, cleans up my cuts and bruises (but still reminds me to be tough); the one who encourages me, calls me beautiful, brushes my hair, loves me unconditionally, and still lets me sit on his lap. He continues to show me what a father should be like so that one day as he walks me down the aisle I will know what a man who loves Jesus, his wife, and kids truly looks like.

There are times when joy and thanksgiving overwhelm my heart—moments when I see him smile, make jokes, and talk without his teeth in. (By the way, here's a little secret: we have given my dad the nickname "JK Swag" when he doesn't wear his prosthesis. Half of my dad's upper jaw and most of his teeth were removed, so he has a fake set that fills in all that's missing. I will admit, sometimes I understand JK Swag more than I understand JK!) It's in these moments when I have found myself thanking God over and over again for blessing me with my dad. And then there were times when it took every fiber in my body to just get out of bed and prepare to spend the entire day at the hospital with Daddy, knowing that he didn't have a good night. Moments when I would yell and beg God to just make things okay and rescue my dad from this disease.

I don't know what tomorrow holds, but in this moment I choose to trust the God who holds tomorrow with all that I don't know. Having watched my dad struggle and fight through cancer has motivated and inspired me to celebrate Father's Day every day because my father is alive! God is not finished with him yet. Knowing this truth, I choose to rejoice in every little detail. When he smiles, we celebrate! When he laughs, we laugh. And when he cries, so do we as we thank God for every tear.

Through this God has taught me to rejoice and thank Him in all circumstances—no matter what. God has given me life on this day. He has given you life on this day. I am determined not to waste one breath or one tear. To run with perseverance the race marked out for me. To live a life of unconditional love for those God has placed in my world. And as I sit here and reflect on my dad's many hospital days, and all the pain, anger, frustration, and hurt, I am so thankful for the chemo, radiation, hospitals, nurses, doctors, fluids, medicine—even the feeding tubes and suction machines. I am thankful for every moment I was able to spend by my dad's side taking care of him.

And so today, I rejoice! I rejoice because even in the midst of sorrow and joy that walk hand in hand, God is still good and my daddy is here, alive. I thank God for blessing me with another day, where I am able to wake up, watch *Sports Center* with my dad, then go for a walk with him, maybe play some cards and read the Bible. Every moment, big or small, is significant because each one is a gift. Today, I will not only rejoice, but I will also cry. Because it's okay. It's okay to cry. And I'm convinced that tears aren't meant for the weak, but for the strong. They too are a gift!

by faith...

Tears are a treasure so incredibly valuable in God's sight that He puts them in a bottle and chronicles our heartbreak. They are not a sign of weakness, but honesty and reality. Hurts and injustice will come to all of us, so putting on a brave face is way overrated and can ultimately cause more harm than good. Better that we should pour our hearts out to God in prayer, and when we're hurt, act like it.

Those who sow in tears will reap with songs of joy.
—Psalm 126:5

You keep track of all my sorrows.
You have collected all my tears in your bottle.
You have recorded each one in your book.
—Psalm 56:8, NLT

Tears are the diamonds of heaven.
—Charles Haddon Spurgeon[1]

From infancy to old age the record of every man's life is written in letters of tears.
—M. R. DeHaan[2]

The tears…streamed down, and I let them flow as freely as they would, making of them a pillow for my heart.
—Augustine[3]

[1] Charles Haddon Spurgeon, *Morning and Evening*, Daily Bible Study, http://dailystudybible.com/Morning_November_3.htm, accessed February 23, 2015.

[2] M. R. DeHaan, MD, *The Chemistry of the Blood* (Grand Rapids, MI: Zondervan Publishing House, 1973), 130.

[3] St. Augustine, *Confessions* IX, 12.

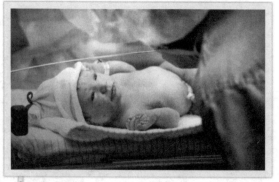

Me looking at Daddy as he's talking to me
in the delivery room May 4, 1995.

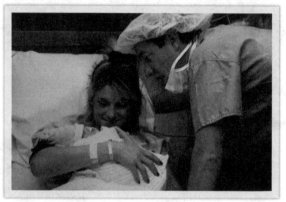

Mommy holding me for the first time.

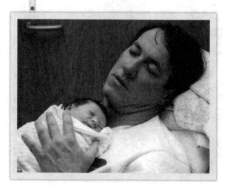

Taking a nap with Daddy.

Mommy holding me at her wedding.

Rockin' a Bills outfit before I even knew
what football was.

TOUCHDOWN! Go Bills!

Trying my Dad's helmet on.

Ready to watch our team play!

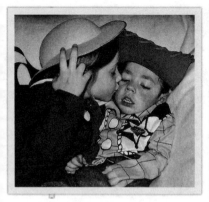

Kissing Hunter.

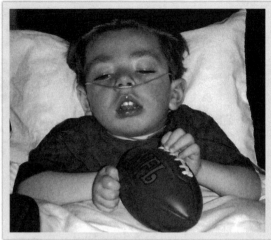

My hero, Hunter, learning the Kelly football grip.

While we are blessed beyond measure to be able to show love, Hunter could only "be" love—and the power in that eclipses even the best everyday expressions of love.

Face-painting fun.

1st Day of first grade, 2001.

Daddy being silly.

Daddy giving a pre-game pep
talk to my basketball team.

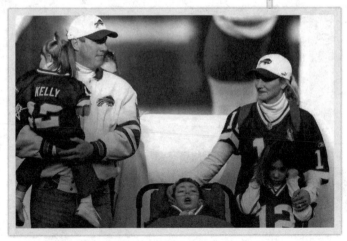

Walking on the Buffalo Bills field when my dad's name
was placed on the Wall of Fame.

Love is about value and the way you show this to the people who have the most value to you. Like anything, if it's worth a lot, you'll make the sacrifice, and so we are usually willing to invest sacrificially in the lives of those we love.

Powder Puff game senior year - Daddy coaching.

A kiss from one of the most important men in my life on my high school graduation day.

Me and Daddy with my over 1,000 points basketball award.

Writing my prayer - Jerusalem,
Wailing Wall, 2014.

Tucking a prayer for my dad into a crevice
of the Wailing Wall in Jerusalem.

Prayer is a gift, but the greater gift is the One to whom we pray, the One who made prayer possible—the One who longs to have a relationship with us and laid down His life in order to make sure He could.

Overlooking the Wailing Wall in Jerusalem.

We wanted the social media world to pray for my dad so we created this hashtag and shared it with everyone.

After #KellyTough went viral a close friend sent my dad this blanket while he was in the hospital.

My dad's jersey hanging in a store window in our local mall.

My dad and Jason a few weeks before Jason died.

After Daddy got hooked up to his feeding tube for the first time, he decided to make the best of it and write Baileys (for Bailey's Irish Creme) on his food container.

Bruce Smith, Andre Reed, and Thurman Thomas came to hang out and say goodbye to my dad before he left for NYC for surgery and treatments.

A moment of prayer with Frank Reich, Dad, Uncle Danny, my mom and me.

Daddy taking his IV medications in an airport while waiting for his flight.

Daddy and Dan Marino in NYC hospital. Mr. Marino brought my dad a huge box of stone crabs, and he made Dad smile and laugh.

Hospital room reminders.

In the midst of joy and sorrow, I have come to understand that every tear tells a story. Every time we weep it's linked to a feeling, a hurt, a laugh, a moment embroidered by God into the tapestry of our lives.

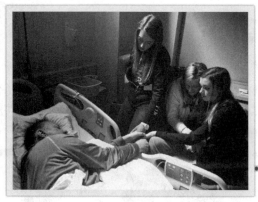

Me, Mom, and Camryn holding Daddy's hand and praying. I'll never forget how much pain my dad was in before he started his treatments.

Writing verses on poster paper to put up around my dad's hospital room.

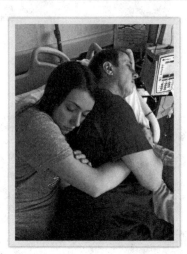

I remember this moment as if it were yesterday. My dad was in so much pain. The doctors had a hard time coming up with a mix of medications that would help him. It was horrible watching him suffer. All I could do was hug him and pray.

In the hallway at the hospital in NYC enjoying some chocolate covered strawberries sent to us from a friend.

Uncle Danny and my dad in NYC after his biopsies.

The view from my dad's Lenox Hill Hospital room in NYC.

Daddy and Thurman Thomas putting together the elephant puzzle at Lenox Hill Hospital in NYC.

Me, Daddy and Bruce Smith working on a puzzle together.

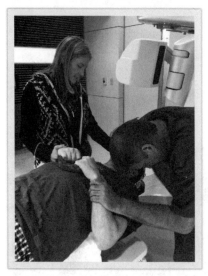

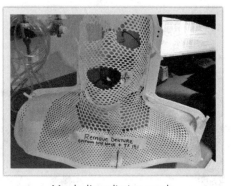

My dad's radiation mask.

Mom and Uncle Ed, Daddy's older brother,
praying before a radiation treatment in NYC.

My dad getting his mask bolted to the table
so he couldn't move during his treatment.

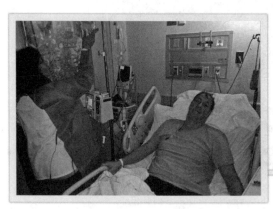

My dad's first chemotherapy treatment in NYC.

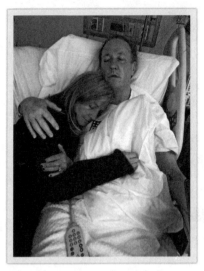

My mom was always there
taking care of my dad.

Camryn and me waiting in my dad's hospital room
in Buffalo while my parents flew back from NYC.

Our moments of waiting were rooted in our
confidence in the One who was holding my
father's very life in His hands.

My parents on their way back home to Buffalo!
A huge day for my dad!!

Daddy and Uncle Ray after Daddy shaved his head for the first time.

A kiss right after he shaved his head; I wanted to shave mine too but my dad wouldn't let me.

Uncel Pat, Uncle Danny, Daddy's best friend, Dave Arnst, Grandpa Kelly, and Uncel Ray - celebrating the shaving of their heads.

Just a few of the amazing nurses who helped take care of my dad.

A quick family picture before my dad went in for his final radiation treatment.

Last chemo treatment in Buffalo!

Last day of radiation - Praise the LORD!

A bunch of friends and family members were waiting to surprise my dad after his final radiation treatment.

Classic Daddy thumbs up pose before going in for 12 biopsies after he had completed all of his chemo and radiation treatments.

Daddy with his radiation doctor, Dr. Shah.

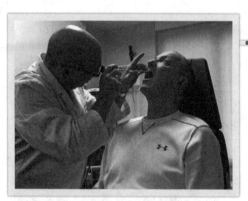

Daddy getting a check-up from Dr. Costantino.

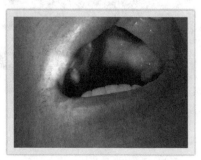

Inside my dad's mouth where they removed the cancer.

God has taught me to rejoice and thank Him in all circumstances—no matter what. God has given me life on this day. He has given you life on this day.

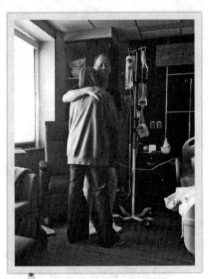

When Daddy asked
Mommy to dance.

When my mom surprised my dad in her
wedding dress for their 18th wedding
anniversary - May 18th, 2014, ECMC
Hospital, Buffalo, New York.

Your teammates (most especially your family)
are all here supporting and fighting
with/for you. But you are still the leader and
always will be! Now is not the time to back
down, no matter the circumstances.

Mom and I giving Daddy a
foot massage.

Daddy and Cam snuggling in the hospital.

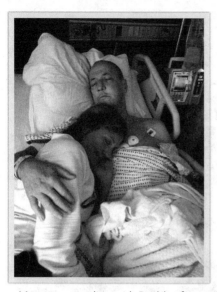

Mommy snuggling with Daddy after his biopsies to confirm that the cancer was gone.

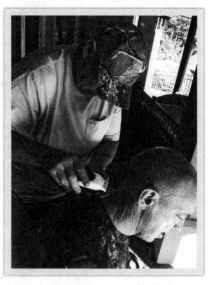

Uncle Ray trimming my dad's hair.

I love him! And we both love Buffalo Bills football.

My interview with Chris Berman, ESPN for Father's Day 2014.

Sometimes the threshold of the race that is run and the fight of faith that is fought rests not on how much faith you have in the promises of God, but rather on how faithful He is to them.

My dad throwing the ball at his football camp - 2014.

A small portion of the cards, prayers, and well wishes my dad received.

Messages on Daddy's bathroom mirror at home; They're still there to this day.

The support for my dad and our family from the Western New York Community and Buffalo Bills fans across the country was amazing!

My parents with Jackson at the Hunter's Hope Family and Medical Symposium 2014 - Kelly Tough theme.

Daddy and his balloon message to Hunter.

Writing a message to Hunter on a red balloon at the Hunter's Hope Family & Medical Symposium 2014.

Hanging out together at home Summer 2014.

All of us having fun again together in Hilton Head after Daddy got the good news that he was cancer free again.

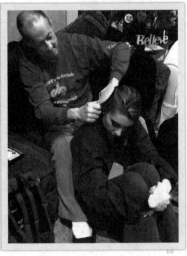

He still brushes my hair.

He still reminds me how to
do the "Kelly" grip.

> If God is good—if His character is
> goodness—then He's good regardless of our
> circumstances. And while it may not be
> easy to embrace, I'm reminded of the reality
> that even if the results weren't good,
> God still is!

Christmas 2014.

Daddy at the cemetery
Christmas day 2014.

Chapter 9

ooo

NOT AFRAID
TO DIE

'm not afraid to die."

The first time I heard those words I was sitting next to my mom in a lackluster New York City hotel room during a media interview with my father. My dad's response to the correspondent's poignant question burned with resolve and conviction, yet it was tempered by such an unexpected tenderness and humility that my mom and I both looked at each other and started to cry.

If he hadn't meant it, it would have been a different story, but the words came from his soul. Suddenly, my whole world fell beneath a shadow, awash in a hazy gray ambiguity that obscured black from white. Questions and confusion began to bombard my heart and mind: *Death? What does he mean he's not afraid to die? Who said he's going to die? No one said that! Or at least I haven't heard the doctors or anyone even come remotely close to that conclusion.* Immediately my guard was up, and I was ready to contend with whoever decided that this could be a potential outcome for my father.

He was in tremendous pain and wasn't feeling well at all, and, truthfully, I didn't think he should do the interview to begin with. He should be sleeping or resting, not talking to the media. Tears began to well up in my eyes as I stared in disbelief. "No...*no*! This is not going to end in death." My mind began to battle back and forth, fear and faith vying to win the day and rule my will. The moment I thought faith won, fear slithered back in. It was exhausting—both mentally and physically.

Although I was frustrated, confused, and on the brink of falling apart, this proved to be one of the most significant moments throughout this entire journey of watching my father. It changed me. Rattled me. And yet, it set my feet on solid ground. I knew that death was a possibility—at least in the most distant corners of my mind I knew that it was. However, I didn't dare wander in those shadowy places. I wouldn't. I couldn't. Because if I did, I was certain the despair would swallow me, and that would be the end of it. I'd lose my toughness, bravery, and hope in an instant.

And yet, that was exactly what I needed. I needed to lose all the mental and emotional toughness I thought I had. Because the moment it was gone, it wasn't my fight anymore. It was God's. He intervened and became the strength I desperately needed in the months that would follow. It wasn't until death became a possible reality for my dad that I was reminded that life is a certainty. Not life on earth, but life beyond earth, beyond the end of time in eternity.

After slipping out to allow myself a brief moment to embrace that place of pain, I returned to the hotel room, my dad's interview, and reality. A reality that was no longer in my comfort zone. In fact, it was a complete war zone. I could no longer mask the truth of death. I could no longer avoid the obvious—my father's health was quickly fading and he might not be able to overcome what was stacked against him.

I needed to lose
all the mental and
emotional toughness
I thought I had.
Because the moment
it was gone, it wasn't
my fight anymore.
It was God's.

Though my years aren't many, I've lived long enough to know full well that the next heartbeat is not promised to anyone, and each breath is a gift—to be unwrapped with gratitude and never to be taken for granted. I am well aware that as sure as the sun rises to bring forth a new day, filled with promise, among those promises is the assurance that we will all die someday. We will. Whether we like or not, death comes to all of us.

I first experienced this when my brother, Hunter, died at just eight and a half years old. I remember that day as if it were yesterday—every feeling, every tear as joy intertwined with tremendous pain in a bittersweet embrace. Joy because I knew my brother wasn't suffering anymore. Pain because I miss him with every breath I breathe. I didn't want my brother to die and I don't want my father to die either. But, I know that death is real and lays claim to each of us—whether we age out of this life and into the next or something intrudes to violate the natural order of things to take us earlier. However, I believe there is something more real than death. Something greater. Something stronger. Something more powerful. Life!

Before I dive into what might be uncharted waters for some of you, I'd like to make a few things clear: I'm not going to tell you what to believe. I'm not even remotely suggesting that I've got this all figured out. What I am going to do is share the source of my hope—a hope that is greater than me, greater than my dread, and greater than our most fierce enemy: death itself. It's a hope that resonates with reality, and brings the most heartwarming colors to the darkest valley, driving away its shadows. A hope I've found in the midst of my father's battle to stay alive so he can walk me down the aisle one day, even if he has to crawl to do it.

In the Bible, in John 14:6, Jesus said unequivocally, "I am the way and the truth and the life. No one comes to the Father except through me." The Bible is not a book about religion; it's a book about relationship. It's the greatest nonfiction story ever told about man's deepest need and God's perfect fulfillment of that need. It's about life and death and the Creator who is beyond both holding all things together in time and eternity for His glory and our good. First John 5:12 clarifies what true life is: "Whoever has the Son has life; whoever does not have the Son of God does not have life."

My dad isn't afraid to die because he knows and trusts the Author of Life—God. It's that simple, and yet, it's the most important thing for us to contemplate and conclude. He has "life" now, and when he takes his last breath on earth, eternal life in heaven—not because of anything my father has done, but solely because he trusts in what Jesus already did for him. Trusting in a God who is greater than our circumstances, greater than our very lives, isn't merely a religious experience or a reason to go to church, it is an ever-present, active reality that is meant to be lived out one day at a time and, as my mom would say, "One prayer at a time."

My dad and I, we've been changed. As a result of the reality and fear of death we had both experienced, we have been ushered into an even greater reality. One that has taken the sting out of death because of the One who conquered it to give us life here and for all eternity.

Sometimes fear looms larger than fact, but it's never larger than faith! I can't stand up to death on my own—it would own me! But in my weakness, I can stand in Christ's victory over it. And that makes me more than Kelly Tough because I'm not afraid of dying. But, to be honest with you, I am afraid of living life without my father. Afraid of what it would be like to have someone else walk me down the aisle on my wedding day. Afraid of what it would be like to watch my mother wake up every morning with-

Sometimes fear looms larger than fact, but it's never larger than faith! In my weakness, I can stand in Christ's victory over death. And that makes me more than Kelly Tough because I'm not afraid of dying.

out her husband by her side. Afraid of not hearing his voice across the room when he takes his teeth out and makes me laugh hysterically. Afraid to lose the most important man in my life.

But I don't live in this place. I don't live in fear because I believe that "perfect love casts out all fear" (1 John 4:18). I believe that God is greater than my deepest, darkest moments. He meets me right where I am, loves me, and works it all together for good. God has brought me back to the place where I'm celebrating each heartbeat and cherishing every moment that I get to spend with my dad. If that means sitting in a tree stand all day, listening to '70s music, or watching ESPN and hunting shows until the sun goes down, that's exactly what I will do. And I know that the instant my father takes his last breath here on earth, he will be in heaven throwing touchdown passes to my brother, Hunter, the one who showed him the true meaning of Kelly Tough.

by faith...

Because life is greater than death, and Jesus, the Giver of life, has actually become a man and vanquished death, we can face and defy any circumstance that confronts us. Even when our challenges loom larger than we are, our peace is in knowing the God who is greater than even death itself. And because He gives us His victory, we can put all our trust in His promise above every challenge that tries to overcome us.

All the days ordained for me were written in your
book before one of them came to be.
—Psalm 139:16

"Death has been swallowed up in victory."
"Where, O death is your victory?

Where, O death is your sting?"
The sting of death is sin, and the power of sin is
the law. But thanks be to God! He gives us victory
through our Lord Jesus Christ.

Therefore, my brothers, stand firm. Let nothing
move you. —1 Corinthians 15:54–58

Chapter 10

○ ○ ○

BACK TO THE 716

April 19, 2014, the day everything changed.

Home...

There really is no place like it. But is that all it is? A place? A hunk of random real estate where we find refuge with family and shut out the world? A piece of geography where we plant our flag? That was all this four-letter word meant to me—until tragedy, heartache, and pain shattered my definition.

I've lived in Buffalo, New York, my entire life. And despite our record-breaking snowfalls and our struggling hockey and football franchises, I'm proud to be a Buffalonian. I know I speak on behalf of the entire Kelly family when I say, there's no place we'd rather be. But, the truth is, it wasn't the Buffalo wings, beef on weck [a sandwich you can't get anywhere else], Niagara Falls, or even Ralph Wilson Stadium that birthed this undying love—it was the people.

Home is nothing without family. And that's exactly what Buffalo is: family. I didn't realize this until my father's cancer treatment for squamous cell carcinoma of the oral and sinus cavity took him far away to a big hospital in the Big Apple. Far from home and everything familiar. Far from One Bills Drive and the die-hard fans we've come to know and love.

I'll never forget the moment when I was faced with the fear of losing the most important man in my life. The one whose strong but gentle hands hold me when I cry. The one who instilled in me a passion for football, sports and life. The man who will one day walk me down the aisle. The one who always reminds me to never give up—to be Kelly Tough.

If cancer was going to take my father to New York City, then I was going to be right there with him. During the second semester of my first year in college, I traveled from Lynchburg, Virginia, to New York City to be with him every weekend as he received his chemotherapy and radiation treatments. During that dark time, his strength and will to survive were slowly fading. And even though I was afraid, I knew my dad would never give up. He couldn't. Because I need him. Our family needs him. The people of Buffalo need him.

On April 19, 2014, everything changed. From a hospital in New York City's Upper East Side to a hospital in Buffalo, New York—from death to life. Everything changed the moment my father found out that he was coming home to finish his treatments. Why? Because although he would spend the next month in the hospital, he knew family, friends and fans would surround him. It was the people. The prayers, the letters, the pictures, the signs, the T-shirts—everything that inspired and encouraged a man who lived to inspire and encourage others.

It may sound cliché, but home really is where the heart is. And our hearts will always be with the City of Buffalo.[1]

---

[1] "What my father's cancer taught me about home," Erin Kelly, Nov. 13, 2014, http://www.nfl.com/news/story/0ap3000000427673/article/what-my-fathers-cancer-fight-taught-me-about-home. I wrote this piece for NFL.com when the NFL Network aired a segment about my dad on national television after he was declared cancer free.)

This was the turning point, the last-minute audible that shifted the momentum of the game, the day everything changed. I had never been so excited to be standing in a hospital room. Camryn and I anxiously peeked around the corner every few seconds to make sure we were prepared to surprise Daddy when he got there. Grammie and Grandpa waited inside room 1021, ready to get pictures and video of his arrival. My mother, sister, and I strategically chronicled unforgettable moments on our social media outlets—and this was certainly one of them. Our homemade *Welcome home, Daddy!* sign was all set, and Cam and I couldn't wait a second longer to see him.

As his wheelchair pulled around the corner of the tenth floor at Erie County Medical Center, after spending over six weeks at Lenox Hill Hospital in the Upper East Side of Manhattan, New York City, I knew that nothing would be the same. Yes, he would have to continue his medical protocols and chemotherapy and radiation treatments. But not even that could shake the joy of being back in Buffalo.

It's true. There's no place the Kelly family would rather be than "the 716" (our phone area code). It's home. It's where our people are; where the team and the fans rally. It's where people we don't even know come up to us in the grocery store and say, "We're praying for you." If Buffalo, New York, is where you call home, you know exactly what I'm talking about. And although people usually give me crazy looks when I tell them I'm from Buffalo, there's really no place I would rather be.

I believe that this overwhelming love for my city and community was shaped out of the deep heartache that my family experienced during the life and death of my brother as well as my dad's cancer battle. I've always loved western New York, but never as much as I do now. And I've never witnessed people come

My longing for comfort has been transformed into a craving to be seated front row in the will of the Almighty. Often, it is that very place where I'm the most uncomfortable.

together the way they did when my father battled cancer in 2013 and 2014. These aren't the type of people who just rally with you during the good times. Rather, they see your need when you're down for the count, and they pick you up off the ground and hold you up when you can no longer stand on your own.

My father was at that point. In fact, I would even dare to say he was beyond it. Daddy desperately needed someone to help him up—even hold him so he could stand. I had watched as he slowly fell apart. I had experienced firsthand what being away from home looked like for my dad. I hated it. I felt as if we were slowly losing our grip on something we wanted so desperately to hold onto. It's exhausting trying to grab onto something that keeps slipping through your fingers. It was as if the moment I believed we had reached land, the sea came crashing onto shore with its savage undertow to try to pull us back out into the deep and drown our hopes once again.

My family's longing for my dad to be home was nothing in comparison to his own desperation to be there. And out of desperation came determination. My mom was willing to do anything and everything to get my dad back to Buffalo. Because what do you do when the quarterback is sacked with no hopes of him returning to the game? The backup grabs his helmet and runs out onto the field ready for battle. And that's exactly what we did.

My parents flew home from New York City on April 19, 2014, just in time for Easter. What a blessing that was! I remember asking God over and over again to please just allow my dad to come home. The closer it got to the holidays, the more earnestly I begged God to bring him back to Buffalo. I'll admit, part of me prayed out of selfish motives because of the longing I had to have him back home. But the other part of me anxiously prayed because of the desperation and exhaustion I saw in my father's eyes as he lay trapped in a New York City hospital room. He needed to be back in Buffalo—there was no question about it. This monumental play call ended up being the exact one needed to turn the game around.

Maybe you're reading this and the thought of home doesn't birth a sense of peace and comfort. Or maybe you're thinking that you don't have a fan base—people to rally behind you and encourage you when you need it most—but maybe you do. You have family, friends, and a familiar community—people and places that lift your spirits just by being near them because they're significant to you. Not only that, you have a heavenly Father, who right now is cheering for you. He's watching everything as it pertains to your life, and He is behind you and with you. If "home" doesn't feel like what I've been talking about, know that regardless of your circumstances, God sees you and wants to draw you into the comfort of His peaceful presence—no matter where you are. He wants you and me to feel most at home with Him, because in His presence is fullness of joy and pleasures forevermore.

When my father returned to Buffalo, he didn't return to our home; he went to a local hospital for care. But when you know you are close to the people who care about you, it makes all the difference in the world.

My uncle Danny, who called us in the Holy Land to let us know the cancer had returned, is one of those people who made all the difference in the world for us. My dad's younger brother, this father of five, keeps the Kelly ship afloat in the stormiest of seas. During the year my father dealt with cancer, Uncle Dan put his entire life on hold to coordinate all the medical details, help orchestrate all the care, and handle the doctor communications for us. From press releases, to doctor's appointments, to travel arrangements, he took care of everything so my mom could be by my father's side every step of the way.

Not only did he keep my dad's business affairs and personal life going by handling all the logistics, every time we turned around, he was plane hopping to New York City and back to cheer my dad on. A God-fearing man, he was a constant source of faith, hope, and peace when the storm was at its worst. Uncle Dan was in the fire with us and we could never have done it without him!

What deeply impacted my life and something I will never forget were the times when Uncle Danny prayed for my dad. He was sincere, honest, and always grateful to God even when it was hard to be. Whenever he prayed, he thanked God and told Him how much we loved Him. He also prayed for my dad to be healed and that we would all remain encouraged and strengthened in our faith.

Speaking of prayer, I'm reminded as I write this of something absolutely extraordinary. From my dad's first chemotherapy and radiation treatments in New York City on April 8, 2014, until his final radiation treatment in Buffalo on May 28, 2014, we prayed together beforehand every time. The fact that we prayed together isn't what was extraordinary because prayer is what we do—part of who we are. What was amazing was the fact that both the doctor in New York City and the lead doctor here in Buffalo said that in the twenty-plus years that they have been taking care of patients, they had never witnessed anyone pray. Now I'm not sharing this to give us a pat on the back but to draw attention to the fact that if prayer is part of your life, people who don't pray will notice. As we continued to seek God for His strength in our weakness, the doctor in Buffalo, Dr. Shah, eventually asked if he could join us. From that treatment on, it became a free-for-all of prayer, and whoever was in the room at the time from the MDs, to all the technicians, to friends and family members, stormed the throne of grace together!

God often allows
us to journey away
from earthly security.
It's where we face
the hardest of
circumstances that
creates a discomfort
that causes us to
hunger and thirst
for a glimpse of our
heavenly home.

Yet as fantastic and enriching as prayer and the sense of love and belonging we feel being "home" is, both are really just a shadow of what awaits us when this life is over. Our true, forever home is in heaven with God, our family in Christ, and all those near and dear to us we have had to say good-bye to. And prayer, well, we will be with God, so prayer as we know it now will be (as only my mind can try to fathom) actually talking to God—face-to-face with Jesus. I cannot even begin to comprehend what that will be like. And even now, as I try to wrap my heart and mind around it, it's as if God is reminding me to just talk to Him now.

Home. God designed the idea and placed a longing for it in our hearts. The first home Jesus knew at His birth wasn't a house at all, but a feeding trough in a dirty, smelly barn. Still, He was in a home: the arms of His mother and father where He was loved and treasured until they got Him to a dwelling He would call home for the next few decades.

Truthfully, a house isn't always a home and home isn't always in a house. Be that as it may, we feel a sense of security and familiarity in our homes that is reminiscent of the home awaiting us in heaven. While here on earth, however, we would do well to remember that there is never a more secure place to be than in the will and arms of God. It is safer to be in the most precarious position in the world, if God has called you there, than hiding behind bolted doors. If you really want that kind of security, you need to lock yourself in a fortress. A fortress that can never be shaken, regardless of disease, death, and decay.

If the safest place to be is in the will of God, then that's exactly where I will build my foundation. When I originally wrote this, it meant having to sit by my father's side in the hospital day after day for months holding onto his hand, praying like never before. It may mean that life is going to be hard—really hard! But God didn't call us to live a life without pain or hardship. In fact, He tells us that in this world we will face troubles (John 16:33). However, God doesn't abandon us in our weaknesses. Rather, He carries us in the midst of them, guaranteeing to hold fast to the promise that He's good and that nothing is beyond His sovereignty. Kelly Tough, as I have learned thus far in this life's journey, is when you hang on to this reality—the greater God reality and purpose in the face of circumstances so far beyond you that they could bury you alive if you let them—whatever form they may take in your life.

I'm not going to try to figure out the will or sovereignty of my heavenly Father. And I'm certainly not going to try to give a theological explanation of the deep, holy things of God that I cannot fully comprehend. All I can share is what I've experienced as a result of allowing God to reign in my heart and make it His home. My longing for comfort has been transformed into a craving to be seated front row in the will of the Almighty. Often, it is that very place where I'm the most uncomfortable. And yet, there's nowhere I'd rather be.

Home is meant to be a place of comfort and refuge. A place of safety. I've learned that God often allows us to journey away from this place of earthly security. It's where we face the hardest of circumstances that create a discomfort that causes us to hunger and thirst for even a glimpse of our heavenly home. I believe that He allows this to happen to remind us of where we belong, to draw us back into His loving, welcoming arms that reach to us from beyond this world where He is—and where we are most at home.

by faith...

We are not home yet. Those around us who keep our hearts safe, whom we trust and treasure—from family to friends—they are the comforts of home to us. However, as beautiful as that is, it is but a shadow of our true home. Christ left His home in heaven to bring heaven with Him to us. It's His kingdom, found wherever the King reigns, and our ultimate home.

> But our citizenship is in heaven. And we eagerly await a Savior from there, the Lord Jesus Christ, who, by the power that enables him to bring everything under his control, will transform our lowly bodies so that they will be like his glorious body.
> —Philippians 3:20–21

> We fix our eyes not on what is seen, but on what is unseen. For what is seen is temporary, but what is unseen is eternal. —2 Corinthians 4:18

> The most beautiful, pleasurable things one could enjoy here on this earth are only hints and whispers, and omens—mere crayon scribbles on a grocery sack—of even greater, more glorious things. Pleasures on earth are just shadows of their realities in heaven. —Joni Eareckson Tada[1]

> If you read history you will find that the Christians who did the most for the present world were precisely those who thought most of the next.
> —C. S. Lewis[2]

---

[1] Joni Eareckson Tada, *A Place of Healing: Wrestling with the Mysteries of Suffering, Pain, and God's Sovereignty* (Colorado Springs, CO: David C. Cook, 2010), 164.

[2] C. S. Lewis, *Mere Christianity* (New York: HarperOne, 1952, 2009), 134.

Chapter 11

○○○

WHY, GOD?

If they only knew.

If they only knew how much my heart aches.

If they only knew how afraid I really am.

The lights of the cameras were blinding, but I had done this many times before, and I knew the typical protocol you adhere to when doing an interview. You wouldn't have known by the rearranged furniture and strategically placed props, but this particular interview with Chris Berman was shot at the hospital. This segment would be aired on Father's Day of 2014 on ESPN, and that alone had me feeling honored and excited.

After my dad's second go-around with cancer, multiple media outlets were requesting interviews with our family. At first Daddy was reluctant to share, but it didn't take long for him to realize that even in the midst of his greatest struggle ever, he had an opportunity to encourage others going through crisis. Once we agreed to do a few interviews, more and more requests came in—and most of them wanted to talk to me as well as my parents. While I was certainly honored and humbled to be asked, I was also intimidated. I wasn't so sure that I was ready to allow anyone, much less the world (through national media), into my pain. However, I have witnessed my parents time and time again be vulnerable and willing to expose their weaknesses so that through them others will be encouraged. I wanted to be just that in the midst of all that we were going through: an encouragement.

I was not told ahead of time what questions Mr. Chris Berman, the ESPN icon, would ask, but I already knew what my answers would consist of: God, faith, family, and more God. It was that simple. I didn't think twice about it. I believed that God would heal my father, and that even if He didn't, He was still good. And as you might expect, oftentimes in interviews, my God-filled responses usually didn't make it in the final cut and often got dropped on the editing floor.

However, when some of my God references did make the cut, most people's responses were encouraging. "I don't know how you do it. Your faith is incredible! You've gone through so much and you still put all your trust in God." Now, as I recall some of the responses sent to me through social media, my throat begins to tighten and I know that tears aren't far behind. Why?

Although I did and still do believe that God is good even in the midst of heartache, there are moments where even the truth seems like a lie. Moments where I've felt as though truth was mocking my insecure, doubtful, and anxious heart. One moment in particular during my dad's battle drastically altered the way I approach God now in the midst of painful circumstances. It was the day I surrendered trying to have it all together. I gave up holding in the tears and the frustration. I laid it all out before God, bare and broken.

It was May 20, 2014, my dad's last chemotherapy treatment. Mom was texting me updates on how everything was going throughout the day because I was away at school in Lynchburg, Virginia. My planner was bursting at the seams, and even though I was busy with school and surrounded by people, the isolation was agonizing. I felt alone. Vulnerable. Hurting. Desperate for home. With each text from my mother, things seemed to be going from bad to worse for my dad. She said he was vomiting again, getting dehydrated, and that there was a possibility that he might have a serious infection brewing somewhere in his system. The news about my dad and being hundreds of miles from my family certainly didn't help.

The day-to-day busyness was overwhelming—not just physically, but emotionally and mentally. My mind was relentless. Pitched back and forth from question to confusion to wonder and worry. It wouldn't let up. And then all at once, my guard seemed to fail as my spiritual confidence and soul-deep convictions came crumbling down. My sadness quickly turned to frustration and I finally asked God why.

"I just don't get it! Why! Why are You allowing this to happen?"

I wasn't expecting an answer, although maybe I should have. The empty, unfriendly silence was brutal. I needed to get out from under the weight of the heaviness. I was sure I would sink into the darkness and mire of desperation. My tears seemed to be my only rescue and my heart physically ached. I wasn't just sad or upset. I was broken. Broken and scared. Scared of the unknown, scared of what I had no control over. I was scared of tomorrow and the next moment.

And that particular moment found me far from home tearing through my townhouse as untamed as a tornado, searching for my journal. With my mind being tossed like a tempest, and my heart pounding out of my chest, there was only one place I knew to go—Jesus. That's it. And in the fervor of that moment, I wasn't up for a simple conversation. I was exhausted, worn, broken, done.

Although I did and still do believe that God is good even in the midst of heartache, there are moments when even the truth seems like a lie.

God knew my heart's cry; He knew that I was weary of praying, tired of pleading with Him over and over again. It was an endless cycle that kept bringing me to the end of myself, on my face in tears. But maybe, that's exactly where I needed to be. I pulled my journal off the shelf, flipped to a blank page, and anxiously began to put my soul on paper.

Lord, I don't even know what to pray anymore. I ask for the same things every day. You know that I just want Daddy to get better. I've asked for trust. I've asked for faith. I've asked for healing. Lord, please! Where are You?

I'm mad.

I'm sad.

I'm frustrated.

Lord, why?

I don't understand.

Why are You allowing this to happen? When will my dad have endured enough? How many times do I have to come to You, crying out on behalf of Daddy? How many times, Lord?

I don't even know what to pray anymore. I'm in this place between faith and fear. And right now, I feel like fear is winning. Forgive me, Lord, for my doubt.

I'm upset and aching for my daddy.

Please, Lord.

Please.

With tears flowing down my face, I picked up my phone. After talking to God, there was only one person I wanted to talk to: my mom. Not only is she one of the wisest and most godly women I know, she's also my best friend.

I tried to catch my breath long enough to speak the words desperately trying to escape from my mind. I felt like my heart would burst if I didn't. "I don't get it, Mom! I just don't get it! *Why?!* Why is God allowing this to happen to us? I don't understand. When will we have a chance to breathe? When will Daddy be okay? When will we have a moment to just rest?"

She was quick to graciously respond in faith: "Erin, I don't know why. I don't understand. And the crazy thing is, I've been feeling the same things you have. I've been asking the same questions you have. And all that I know is, it's okay. It's okay to ask. It's okay to be afraid. It's okay to doubt. It's okay to cry and scream and get frustrated. It's all going to be okay because no matter what's at the end of all this, God's got this. He's got you. He's got me. And He's taking care of your dad." We continued to talk and cry together, and in those moments I experienced a sense of peace that I had been desperate for.

I'm not afraid to admit that in the midst of my phone call meltdown, I had this feeling that God just might fire back, "Why not, Erin?" But what I felt in that moment and what I knew was real were two very different things. In fact, the only reason I could allow myself to vent my hurt and desperation was because I knew that the Lord could handle the emotional storm raging in me. He understands and loves me, and even if I didn't understand why, I could rest in the reality that He knew why. And because He loves me more than His own life, I could not only rest, but rage as well—He was and is big enough to handle both!

I am convinced that the Lord and source of all reality would rather you and I be real with Him because He knows the depths of our hearts—the things we will never understand—and He loves us unconditionally, regardless. He is big enough to take every demand and doubt we throw at Him, and turn them into

God is going to
use the many
different sorrows
in this life to
reveal His love
for us, deepen our
relationship with
Him, and better form
His Son's image
in our souls.

something beautiful by drawing us closer to Him through our questions and fears. The best relationships are the most honest, where any sort of pretense and posturing is nonexistent. That's the kind of relationship God longs to have with each of us. The kind that is real and authentic, filled with all that is true, noble, praiseworthy, and excellent. One that is free from the poison of self-centeredness, arrogance, and pride.

Don't we want that kind of authenticity in all our relationships? I do. But having the kind of intimacy we're talking about here has to begin with God first. In fact, we can't possibly share the depths of who we are with another human being in a selfless way unless we have come to the end of ourselves. To be honest with you, I'm not even sure exactly what that even looks like when lived out, but I do know that it all has to start with Jesus—His life living in and through us.

Trying to grasp the eternal reasoning behind the earthly tragedies that drive our "whys" can suck the life out of you. It's an exercise in futility! The same is true of trying to reconcile a God we know is love and has all power with life circumstances that appear to contradict that reality. I think Jesus said it best in John 16:33: "I have told you these things, so that in me you may have peace. In this world you will have trouble. But take heart! I have overcome the world."

Trouble, trials, heartbreak—it's a given. And given that given, God is going to use the many different sorrows in this life to reveal His love for us, deepen our relationship with Him, and better form His Son's image in our souls. We may cry out in frustration, "Why, Lord?" But one way or another, what comes back is, "It's enough that I know."

by faith...

Asking why is human, but it is rarely fruitful and oftentimes frustrating. God doesn't owe us an explanation. We were created by Him and for Him; therefore, we are called to surrender to Him without prejudice, conditions, or ultimatums. He is Lord and we are not. His ways are not ours; they are higher, greater, and beyond our finite comprehension. His perfect plans cannot be thwarted and He reasons from an eternal vantage point. Thankfully, however, He loves us without limit! So rather than pretend or go through the motions, hoping that whatever we're feeling will eventually go away, we can come boldly to God without reservation or hesitation. His grace is sufficient for us and His mercies are ever present. As we learn to trust Him, we can still ask questions but also rest in not knowing because we know that He knows.

> Why, O Lord, do you stand far off?
> Why do you hide yourself in times of trouble?
>   —Psalm 10:1

> My God, my God, why have you forsaken me?
> Why are you so far from saving me,
> so far from the words of my groaning?
> O my God, I cry out by day, but you do not answer,
> by night, and am not silent. —Psalm 22:1–2

> Hear my cry, O God;
> listen to my prayer.
> From the ends of the earth I call to you,
> I call as my heart grows faint;
> lead me to the rock that is higher than I.
> For you have been my refuge,
> and a strong tower. —Psalm 61:1–3

Chapter 12

o o o

WAITING

Tuesday, August 19, 2014

Lord, I don't know what You have in store for THIS day. We have been waiting for this day to dawn for the past five months—the day Daddy gets his scans in New York City. And even though it may sound like a Christian cliché, I mean it with all my heart: Thank You that we aren't waiting on a scan, but waiting on You! Waiting on YOU TO DO what only YOU CAN DO. You alone are the Healer! You are greater than our circumstances. You alone can conquer cancer; You give the breath of life and hold the keys of death. My daddy's life is in Your mighty hands. Thank You that in our waiting, You already know and You're already there.

You have given us awesome promises we can trust, because we trust You—You're not just a promise maker, You're a promise keeper. Thank You that Your victory is ours! We have life because of You and we have hope because of You. Even when I don't understand, I trust You, Lord.

I'll never forget that day. It was August 20, 2014. It was as if my world revolved around a single moment, the moment when

He lovingly
revealed to me
the true longing
of my heart—what
I'm really
waiting for:
Him.

my dad would get the scan results we had been waiting for. All I wanted to do was pray, and that's exactly what I did. Although I went about my school day, going in and out of classes, I was in constant communication with God.

Sadly, it turned out that this long-awaited moment would be extended for several more weeks. His initial scans were not conclusive, so more tests were required, which ultimately meant more waiting. More praying. More trusting. More believing. We could have put on a brave face, but instead opted again for reality, hoping to be Kelly Tough in the face of another go-round with obstacles bigger and stronger than we were. Thankfully, they weren't bigger or stronger than God, as reflected in the words my mom shared through her Instagram account:

We have come away from our checkup visit in NYC encouraged and hopeful. Preliminary scan results have necessitated the need for biopsies to be done in order to confirm what we hope to be true...that the cancer has been eradicated. We will not know the outcome until this procedure is completed. And so...we continue to PRAY, rejoice, live...wait and trust GOD who holds ALL things together. God, who is the Alpha and Omega, the Beginning and the End, and every moment in between. In the midst of it all, I know He's got this. Thank you for praying! Thank you for holding us up during this time. We are so grateful for you! #prayersforjk #kellytough.

I've never been so anxious for "good news" and for someone to assure me that my dad's fight with cancer was over, that he was completely healed. I just wanted to know that he was going to be okay. In that moment, that's all I could think about. All I hoped for. My mind flirted with every option in the book. "If the cancer is still in his body, then I'm leaving school and going home. I can't let Mommy do this on her own. And if his body is going to continue to fall apart, I'm going to be there to pick up the pieces and carry him."

Although fear beleaguered my mind, deep down I believed with all my heart that my dad was healed. In the midst of the wondering and waiting, God granted me an indescribable peace. As I think back to this moment, I'm overwhelmed by God's grace. Overwhelmed by how He lovingly revealed to me the true longing of my heart—what I'm really waiting for: Him.

We weren't waiting on a diagnosis, a scan, or a simple phone call from a doctor to tell us the news that our hearts ached to hear—even though we were. Those earthly assurances are fickle and fleeting because someday people will forget the news headline saying, "Jim Kelly Is Cancer Free!" They will. It's the world we live in and that's okay.

Ultimately, it's not about my dad. It's not about being Kelly Tough. It's not about the Kelly family at all. It's about Jesus. If you finish reading this book and only hold onto one thing, let it be this: Jesus.

Our moments of waiting were rooted in our confidence in the One who was holding my father's very life in His hands. The One who has the power to heal and has taken the sting out of death. Although I anticipated hearing the words, "Daddy is healed," I clung even tighter to the Healer.

Before time began, God knew the outcome. He knew all that our family would endure, and He knew we would find our strength in Him alone as a result. Our waiting only caused us to run harder after God. Because in the midst of the unknown, there is an unshakable assurance in the One who knows.

Our waiting only caused us to run harder after God. Because in the midst of the unknown, there is an unshakable assurance in the One who knows.

And so now, in this moment, I am living in the time in between. Each day I wait in expectation of eternity. A place where there is no more pain, suffering, or cancer. A place where every fear, doubt, and worry will fade away in the presence of His perfect love. Every question will be answered, not because God holds all answers (even though He most certainly does), but because He *is* the answer.

My earthly waiting is simply a glimpse of where my heart is destined for, where all my hopes rest: in the arms of Jesus!

by faith...

Waiting is part of life. We all know that things don't always happen how or when we want them to. And the old cliché—"Good things come to those who wait"—well, it's certainly not true every time. However, waiting on God rather than anything or anyone is always worth the wait. It's a sign of trust, an exercise in faithfulness, and an expression of well-placed hope. Whatever response or resolution we are waiting for, it's critical to remember not just *what*, but *who* we're waiting on! Although not bound by it, God created time. Therefore, in all things, in every circumstance, His timing is perfect.

> Give ear to my words, O Lord,
> consider my sighing.
> Listen to my cry for help,
> my King and my God,
> for to you I pray.
> In the morning, O Lord, you hear my voice;
> in the morning I lay my requests before you and
> wait in expectation. —Psalm 5:1–3

> I waited patiently for the Lord;
> he turned to me and heard my cry. —Psalm 40:1

I wait for the Lord, my soul waits,
and in his word I put my hope.
My soul waits for the Lord
more than watchmen wait for the morning,
more than watchmen wait for the morning.
—Psalm 130:5–6

I am still confident of this:
I will see the goodness of the Lord
in the land of the living.
Wait for the Lord;
be strong and take heart
and wait for the Lord. —Psalm 27:13–14
Who hopes for what he already has? But if we hope
for what we do not yet have, we wait for
it patiently. —Romans 8:24–25

God marks across some of our days, "Will explain later."
—Vance Havner[1]

---

[1] Vance Havner, Devotion of the Day, "Not Now but Afterwards,"
www.vancehavner.com/?p=1425.

Chapter 13

o o o

THE GREATER MIRACLE

September 4, 2014, 4:30 p.m.

I don't even have words, I'm speechless—You are so good! Thank You. Thank You for granting the prayers of thousands of people. Thank You for hearing our cry and coming to our rescue. Thank You for healing my daddy. My heavenly Father healed and is healing my earthly father. I'm overwhelmed. It doesn't even seem real. But thank You that it is! And like the doctor said—it's nothing short of a MIRACLE. That's Your nature. You do the unexplainable and the unthinkable. Take all the glory, God—it belongs to You! O Lord, thank You for using our human frailty in the face of adversity to unleash Your strength through us. I am nothing without you. We are absolutely NOTHING without You. And yet with You—we have EVERYTHING we could ever need. Everything!

It felt good not to fight the tears. To just let them mingle with my makeup and stain my cheeks as they cascaded like tinted raindrops on a window. Christian artist Jeremy Camp's epic worship song "He Knows" rang out from my phone and echoed the cry of my heart. It offered a perfect soundtrack that strengthened me as I stood against the set of circumstances threatening our family. It was late summer, almost autumn really. I had just started my sophomore year of college at Liberty University and was nervously awaiting test results.

However, I hadn't taken any academic tests yet. What I was waiting for were the results of my dad's twelve biopsies taken from his oral cavity—biopsy results that would determine the effectiveness of his cancer treatments; results that had been delayed due to more biopsies and tests needed. The emotional and spiritual ground beneath me was shifting and shaking as I anxiously ached for God to come through with the desire of my heart.

Though he had hung up his cleats years ago, because my father was an NFL Hall of Famer, his celebrity status had some serious staying power and his fan base still garnered an incredible show of support. Consequently, the social media rumor mill was infested with hearsay regarding my dad's health and the results of his treatment. I didn't know what to think or believe because a good friend and former teammate of my dad's had inadvertently leaked his test results on Twitter before my parents could actually share them with Cam and me.

As the leaked information and all kinds of innuendo spread across the social media world like wildfire, I didn't know what was true. What I was keenly aware of, thanks to my parents' insight, experience, and instruction, was the potentially cunning nature and possible misdirection common to certain segments of the media. For me, however, the buzz about my father compounded the anguish I was dealing with. He had endured chemo and radiation, and now had undergone the necessary biopsies to determine if the treatment had been successful. And in spite of all the rumors, I was not about to buy into anything unless I heard it straight from my father or mother. So I waited by the phone.

But it wasn't easy. To say I was distracted in class was the understatement of understatements. The only story I wanted to cover in my journalism class was a front-page feature on my dad's negative test results! I sat in my home away from home praying and trying to make sense out of the tweets and texts I was getting congratulating me on my father being "cancer free." I just about wore a trench in the floor from pacing and left skid marks on my phone's keyboard from texting and calling my mother, father, and grandmother trying to verify all the well-wishes I was receiving. In between attempts to contact my family, I prayed as I paced. And it went on like that forever. Nobody was responding and it was driving me crazy.

Finally, I got Grammie on the other end of the phone, but she couldn't shed any light on the results. Knowing I was discouraged and longing to hear my father's voice, Grammie found just the right words as we prayed over the phone. We hung up, and at long last, all the pieces of this puzzle came together.

The telephone rang and…it wasn't my mother, nor was it my father. It was *everyone, and they were all on "speaker"*! I was crying so hard I could hardly speak and was grateful that I had been sitting down as I felt strength drain from me so completely that I might have collapsed had I been standing. My father began explaining that he had talked to his doctor and that the biopsy results had confirmed that the treatment had been successful and *his cancer was gone.*

"Well, I just wanted to tell you that Daddy is free of cancer. Next thing I have to do is, I have to do a couple of follow-ups. But it's such great news and thank God. We are blessed. I am blessed! Yeah, Dr. Costantino said it was nothing short of a miracle. Because he wasn't sure when he went in how it was going to come out, ya know, the biopsies. But they all came back negative. Thank God."

He wanted to tell Cam and me himself, and wanted us all to be together, so it was necessary to wait until he picked my sister up from school.

I understood and loved the fact that my dad wanted to wait and share the amazing news with all of us at the same time. A deep sense of relief and peace filled my heart and mind. I was as wide open and vulnerable as I'd ever been and couldn't stop crying. I thanked God over and over again.

Though miles apart, Mommy, Daddy, Cam, and I shared our tears, and joyful relief—they all came tumbling out as an unguarded act of gratitude. We kept the phone on "speaker," as we talked, cried, and thanked God. But nothing could have prepared us for the powerful prophetic word my mother had shared with my father earlier in the day, and then with all of us on this phone call.

You have to know my mom; her heart is so full, and she extends God's grace and pours forth His love so beautifully. One of the traits I most admire about her is her lack of guile—she's the real deal. I live with her and see her when no one's looking—the sinner and the saint. I watch her win and lose, break it and fix it; I see why she needs a Savior and watch how beautifully He loves her. She's thoroughly grounded and would be as comfortable on the red carpet as she would be picking up our Chihuahua's poop; what you see *really is* what you get with her.

The day my dad shared the incredible news, somewhere tucked within the tension of the pending test results, the Lord had already prepared my mother for the outcome, pouring a peace

The greater miracle
is found in seeking
the Deliverer first
and deliverance
second; in longing
for the Healer even
more than the
healing; pursuing
the Miracle Worker
before pursuing the
miracle—the Giver
before the gift.

that passes all understanding into her heart and mind. A peace from the heart of God that she couldn't wait to share with all of us. You see, just hours before learning the test results, my mother was having her quiet time with God, a daily routine she has faithfully embraced since very early in her Christian walk. During her "QT" that morning, God led her to Psalm 21:1–7, which was written by King David—and several thousand years later, for Jim, Jill, Erin, and Camryn Kelly as well.

> The king rejoices in your strength, LORD.
> How great is his joy in the victories you give!
> You have granted him his heart's desire
> and have not withheld the request of his lips.
> You came to greet him with rich blessings
> and placed a crown of pure gold on his head.
> He asked you for life, and you gave it to him—
> length of days, for ever and ever.
> Through the victories you gave, his glory is great;
> you have bestowed on him splendor and majesty.
> Surely you have granted him unending blessings
> and made him glad with the joy of your presence.
> For the king trusts in the LORD;
> through the unfailing love of the Most High
> he will not be shaken.

My mother's journal entry in response to the verses she read on the day we received the results is very raw and honest. Here is a small portion of her heart's cry:

Are You telling me that You have given us the VICTORY over this?

Are You telling me that You have granted Jim length of days?

To walk his daughters down the aisle, to see his grandchildren?

We have asked You for life; are You telling me that You are giving it?

I want to hold onto this but I'm scared—what if?

Pondering the message in her heart, my mom marshaled all the faith she had and seized the promise. And although she was given a peace that would see her through whatever the results of the biopsy would be, she felt God was giving her and my father very specific prayer answers through the above passages. In the face of a literal life-and-death struggle, He gave answers such as, "He asked you for life, and you gave it to him," and, "How great is his joy in the victories you give! You have granted him his heart's desire and have not withheld the request of his lips."

Not only did my mother quietly treasure these promises in her heart and let them guide her prayers and attitude in the hours immediately before my father's test results were known, but she took the gutsy step of sharing them with the man whose life literally hung in the balance. My mom chose to encourage my dad to trust and believe Psalm 21, to own it and allow his very life to rest upon its promises. To some that would seem pretty thin—but the real world often is. And sometimes the threshold of the race that is run and the fight of faith that is fought rests not on how much faith you have in the promises of God, but rather on how faithful He is to them.

My mother shared her reflections with us all on the phone, capturing the intensity of the moment. "The Lord gave me Psalm 21:1–7 literally hours before we found out the test results," she said, choking back tears. "I read the passage to Daddy after God brought me to it, though at first I was afraid because I didn't want to get his hopes up. The thing is that I was so overwhelmed feeling like God was assuring me that He was giving us the victory over this cancer. But even as I felt like He did, I was still unsure. I wanted to stand on it—yet still felt torn. What if…"

My mom prayed continuously and fervently for Daddy's healing—we all did. But one thing that profoundly struck me in the midst of it all was the realization that she had settled it well beforehand; she was going to live out what she understood to be true: God's heavenly value system, which placed unconditional love in the lordship of Christ was the axis her world revolved around. That was her identity, and I was determined to make it mine as well—because if that's who I was, then everything I did would emerge from that transcendent reality.

My mother's jubilance, gratitude, and praise of God in her journal entry after the revelation of my father's test results are unmistakable:

> BIOPSY RESULTS—NEGATIVE!
> *Absolutely amazing!*
> *Lord, how You prepared me before we knew—through YOUR WORD. Part of Your amazing plan. Lord, Your perfect timing—the opening of the NFL season. It's truly overwhelming! Mind blowing! Humbling! I am stunned by Your mercy and Your grace, Your love, kindness, gentleness, Lord, Your tenderness. "Nothing short of a miracle." That's what Dr. C said.*
> *All Glory to You, Jesus. All Glory!*
> *You're amazing and I long for all to know, see, hear what You have done. All because of You and for You. The Greater Gift and Glory! The Greater Miracle. Before we knew the*

outcome You sent Your peace. You are the praise of all mankind.

The greater miracle is found in seeking the Deliverer first and deliverance second; in longing for the Healer even more than the healing; pursuing the Miracle Worker before pursuing the miracle—the Giver before the gift. My mother is the kind of person whose choices in this life are based upon whether or not they will bring her closer to Christ Himself, as opposed to what He will do for her. And that is the heart I seek, the heart I'm determined to walk in—whatever it may cost. A heart that loves God well beyond anything He can do for me.

With respect to my father, the greater miracle wasn't that the chemotherapy and radiation worked and that my father is now cancer free—although certainly this is a miracle, the one we prayed for. But the greater miracle is everything God did in the midst of it all to reveal Himself, draw us closer to His heart, and radiate His glory.

The greater miracle is growing up in a family with a father who was raised to be Kelly Tough—a daddy who taught me to never give up no matter what, to fight through the pain regardless of how bad it hurts, to give it all you've got despite any and all cost. A father who exemplified what it means to always be tough, and yet came to the realization that it's not about being tough at all, but that our greatest strength is found in and through our greatest weakness.

The greater miracle lies in recognizing that the setbacks in life are actually set-ups for God's grace and mercy to be displayed and magnified in the most unexpected people and places. People like Uncle Ray, whose prayer, though simple and humble, unexpectedly pierced my heart in a way that forever changed

The greater miracle is growing up in a family with a father who was raised to be Kelly Tough—a daddy who taught me to never give up no matter what, to fight through the pain regardless of how bad it hurts, to give it all you've got despite any and all cost.

my relationship with God. And places like a stark hospital room where we met Jason, a man who had just weeks to live but was so full of life and love that he seemed more alive than most people who enjoy perfect health.

Ponder the greater miracle of finding joy in the midst of sorrow and suffering, or in recognizing that weakness is a bridge to the strength and power of God that gives us the ability to be more than conquerors and overcomers. And isn't part of this overcoming and conquering choosing to embrace our responsibility to love and forgive when we think we have the right to do the opposite?

Or the miracle unleashed in truly realizing, like I mentioned above, that our need for the Healer is greater than our need for healing; that the sting of death has been swallowed up in victory because of the One who conquered it to give us life here—and finally fullness of life in eternity; that Christ is and always will be greater and more powerful than cancer. Or it can be found in the greater miracle that although none of us know what tomorrow holds, in this moment we can choose to trust the God who holds tomorrow and all that we don't know. And what about embracing the truth that we don't have to have it all together, because God treasures and accepts you and me right where we are. And that our mess of imperfections is the very place where Jesus redeems our brokenness, transforming and perfecting it into something absolutely beautiful.

Unquestionably, the greater and more compelling miracle is God's endgame—His loving us so completely and unconditionally that He gave His One and Only Son so we might be reconciled to Him. God destroyed every power and principality that would try to stand against His love for the crown of His creation—humanity—you and me. And nothing in time or eternity can force us from His loving embrace, undo the work of the cross, or put

Christ back in the grave. Romans 8:38–39 assures us, "For I am convinced that neither death nor life, neither angels nor demons, neither the present nor the future, nor any powers, neither height nor depth, nor anything else in all creation, will be able to separate us from the love of God that is in Christ Jesus our Lord." We can trust Him because there is nothing in time or eternity that can ever undo His victory over sin and death, or separate us from God's greater miracle—knowing Him through His Son, Jesus.

by faith...

We all have wounded hearts, deep needs (physical, emotional, and spiritual), lives to live, and dreams to seek! However, thanks to the Spirit of God indwelling us, we can fix our eyes on the greater and more compelling passion— the Healer above the healing, the Giver above the gift, the Truth above truths. This is the greater miracle: we are unconditionally accepted as a part of God's family through Christ.

> I will boast all the more gladly about my weaknesses,
> so that Christ's power may rest on me. That is why,
> for Christ's sake, I delight in weakness, in insults, in
> hardships, in persecutions, in difficulties. For when I
> am weak, then I am strong. —2 Corinthians 12:9–10

Do I believe with all my heart and soul that if my dad was not healed, if the cancer did come back, that God is still who He says He is—that He's still good? If I believe that to be true, I will live differently.

Chapter 14

○ ○ ○

GOODNESS BEYOND
OUR CIRCUMSTANCES

F ear is too simple. It's just too easy—you let go and fall into its cold, dark embrace that always seems to be waiting with arms wide open. I fall into it without even realizing that I'm paralyzed in its grasp. And you know the old saying, "It's not the fall, but the landing that gets you"—boy, is that ever true. The faster I fall the harder it is to get up.

The past few days I've been especially fearful and anxious. Maybe it's because I'm starting a new semester and I'm away from my family again. Maybe it's because the homework is already piling up faster than snow in Buffalo. Or maybe it's just because it's that time again—time for my dad, Mom, and Uncle Danny to fly to New York City, then drive to Lenox Hill Hospital to meet with Dr. C and his team again, and get new scans to confirm that the cancer is still gone.

It's Wednesday, January 21, 2015, and in about two months it will mark one year since our family found out that my dad had oral cancer for the second time. My mind must associate this time of year with his diagnosis because I can feel its despair weighing heavily upon my heart. Since we received the news that he was cancer free back in September of 2014, I haven't worried as much about him or what the results would be. Maybe because living under the cloud of such an ominous threat has caused us to treasure every moment for the sacred gift it is and live each day as if it's our last.

And yet recently I've allowed worry to silently slither in, causing my faith to falter beneath a burden that strips away my joy and gratitude for all that God has done—for all that He is. However, every fear was shattered about ten minutes ago when I received a text from my mom saying that all the scans came back negative—my dad is still cancer free! There are no words to describe the mix of emotions surging through me right now. I'm completely overwhelmed by God's outrageous mercy, provision, and faithfulness...overwhelmed by all the precious people who continue to garrison the Kelly family with prayer.

As I scroll through Twitter and Instagram, I'm profoundly humbled by everyone's sincere and encouraging comments. And though this strengthens my heart, there are three simple yet profound words that are convicting me in the most loving yet penetrating manner: "God is good!" I've spoken these words or heard them from someone else countless times. And yet, the only time I can recall saying or hearing them is after something good actually happens.

What strikes me about this is that if God is good—if His character is goodness—then He's good regardless of our circumstances. And while it may not be easy to embrace, I'm reminded of the reality that *even if the results weren't good, God still is!* Do I believe with all my heart and soul that if my dad was not healed, if the cancer did come back, that God is still who He says He is—that He's still good? If I believe that to be true, I will live differ-

Today I will not
be shaken by fear
or doubt or worry.
And tomorrow I
will rejoice in every
heartbeat as if it's my
last, one breath at a
time, and one prayer
at a time, because
God is good.

ently. Maybe better stated, I will live abundantly. I will be fearless, walking in His goodness through the worst, most devastating circumstances. I will praise Him in the storm because He walks on water and calms the wind to a hush.

And so today I choose to stand firmly upon this reality—God is good whether my dad is cancer free or not. Today I praise and thank Him because my dad is alive and continuing to heal every day. Today I thank God that He isn't finished with us yet. He began a good work in us and will be faithful to complete it. Today I will not be shaken by fear or doubt or worry. And tomorrow I will rejoice in every heartbeat as if it's my last, one breath at a time, and one prayer at a time, because God is good. When I rest in the truth that the God who is good, even when my circumstances are not, is also love, then I can live in the reality that His perfect love will drive out all fear, just as 1 John 4:18 promises! With this I pray…

Lord, I come before You today with my heart wide open. I know no other way but to come to You with all that I am in this moment. I lay my fear, doubt, worry, and heartache at Your feet. You alone are mighty to save. You are sovereign and omnipotent, working all things together for our good and Your glory. You hold today, tomorrow, and eternity in Your hands, working out a perfect plan for all creation that cannot be thwarted. While circumstances all around me change like shifting sand, You stay the same—incapable of being anything other than what You are: gracious, merciful, loving, kind, and always GOOD!

Because of You…

I am saved.

I am changed.

I am chosen.

I am loved.
I am forgiven.
I am free.
I am fearless.
I am more than a conqueror.
I am an overcomer.
I am redeemed.
I am strong and courageous.
I am victorious.
I am…Kelly Tough.

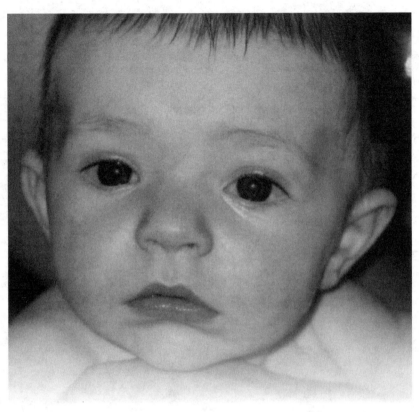

preventing needless deaths...
newborn screening advocacy

helping suffering children & families...
family care

finding a cure...
leukodystrophy research

giving hope...
where there is none

HUNTER'S HOPE

www.huntershope.org

Appendix A

○ ○ ○

ABOUT
HUNTER'S HOPE

Hunter's Hope was founded in 1997 by Pro Football Hall of Fame quarterback Jim Kelly and his wife, Jill, after their infant son, Hunter (February 14, 1997–August 5, 2005), was diagnosed with Krabbe leukodystrophy. Krabbe is a rare, fatal, genetic disorder that affects the central and peripheral nervous systems. Children affected by Krabbe suffer greatly and typically do not live beyond their second birthday.

Hunter's Hope was established to address the acute need for information and research with respect to Krabbe disease and related leukodystrophies. In addition, we strive to support and encourage those afflicted and their families as they struggle to endure, adjust, and cope with the demands of these fatal illnesses.

Accordingly, our mission is fourfold:

- To broaden public awareness of Krabbe disease and other leukodystrophies, thus increasing the probability of early detection and treatment.

- To gather and provide current, functional information and service linkages to families of children with leukodystrophies.

- To fund research efforts that will identify new treatments, therapies, and, ultimately, a cure for Krabbe disease and other leukodystrophies.

- To establish an alliance of hope that will nourish, affirm, and confront the urgent need for medical, financial, and emotional support of family members and those afflicted with leukodystrophies.

Among these essential goals, founders Jim and Jill Kelly seek to inspire an appreciation of all children and express a thankful heart toward God for these precious gifts of life.

Since the inception of Hunter's Hope, countless lives have been touched by bringing awareness to these devastating diseases, funding research to improve treatment options for those affected by leukodystrophies through the Hunter James Kelly Research Institute, and providing support and hope to over seven hundred affected families as they cope with these devastating diseases. Additionally, thousands of newborns have benefited nationally through the foundation's work to advocate for early detection through newborn screening for diseases that, like Krabbe, are not otherwise clinically recognizable at birth.

For more information, please visit our website at www.huntershope.org. You can also follow us on social media:

Facebook – www.facebook.com/HuntersHope
Twitter – @HuntersHopeFDN
Instagram – @HuntersHopeFDN
YouTube – www.youtube.com/HuntersHope

ABOUT
KRABBE LEUKODYSTROPHY

Krabbe (crab-ay) disease is one of over forty identified leukodystrophies, an inherited group of disorders of the white matter in the brain, affecting one in seven thousand individuals. Onset of symptoms can occur in the first months of life through adulthood, inducing a sudden loss of abilities such as voluntary movement and speech, and result in severe morbidity and death.

Krabbe disease affects both the central and peripheral nervous systems, which are responsible for all of the body's voluntary and involuntary movements. The central nervous system is made up of the nerves within the brain and spinal cord and is the primary control center of the body. The peripheral nervous system's primary function is to carry information from the brain and spinal cord throughout the body to the limbs and organs.

Early infantile Krabbe disease is the most severe form and is often initially misdiagnosed as colic, reflux, food/milk allergy, or even cerebral palsy. Affected babies begin to show symptoms, including severe irritability, feeding issues, stiffness, and unmet developmental milestones, within the first months of life.

Symptoms: general irritability (excessive crying), stiffness, decline in motor skills, loss of previously attained milestones, difficulty in feeding, seizures, arching of the back, jerking of the arms and/or legs.

Those with late-onset Krabbe disease begin to show symptoms between six months and three years of age. Symptoms are the same as those described in early infantile Krabbe disease.

Symptoms: general irritability (excessive crying), stiffness, decline in motor skills, loss of previously attained milestones, difficulty in feeding, seizures, arching of the back, jerking of the arms and/or legs.

JUVENILE-ONSET KRABBE DISEASE AND ADULT-ONSET KRABBE DISEASE

Those with juvenile-onset Krabbe disease typically show an initial regression of motor skills at three years of age or later. After the initial decline, the disease progresses slowly, often lasting years.

Adult-onset Krabbe disease often results in initial vision problems, generally followed by muscle stiffness and difficulty walking. It is possible that adult-onset Krabbe disease can be misdiagnosed as multiple sclerosis.

ABOUT
NEWBORN SCREENING

Newborn screening is a state-based program that looks for serious developmental, genetic, and metabolic disorders that would not otherwise be detected. For these diseases, early detection and treatment is essential to preventing irreversible mental or physical disabilities, even death.

Just after birth, a few drops of blood are taken from a baby's heel and placed on a card that is sent to the state's newborn screening lab. The results are then sent to the baby's pediatrician and the hospital where they were born. Newborn screening does not diagnose diseases, but identifies which babies need additional testing to confirm or rule out these diseases. Although rare, such diseases are treatable if caught early.

Appendix B

o o o

THE ROMANS ROAD

Walking the Path that Leads from Death to Life

There have been a number of verses that have helped me understand the road to salvation. Commonly referred to as the Romans Road, there is a sequence of passages taken from the book of Romans that show the path to salvation, leading from death to life. These Scripture references succinctly explain man's desperate condition and God's loving response to it.

The truth is that people don't usually like to talk about sin. In fact, the world spends more time glorifying sinful behavior than good behavior. But the truth is, we were all born sinful, leading self-centered lives by nature. You don't believe me? Just look at a two-year-old when she cries, "Mine!" and takes a toy away from the boy she is playing with.

Sin dominates our hearts, thinking, and decision-making, ultimately separating us from God. Our proclivity to sin is part of who we are. Ever since Adam and Eve in the garden of Eden, it is in our DNA. Paul writes to the Romans, reminding them of this fact: "For all have sinned and fall short of the glory of God" (Romans 3:23).

The road to redemption, or any sort of recovery for that matter, starts with recognizing our desperate need. In this case, we are born sinners. In Adam we have all been born under the weight of sin, and we need someone to rescue us from that sin because we are powerless and cannot save ourselves from it. When we recognize our need, we can then admit that we are sinful and fall short of God's glory and His perfect desire for humanity.

"What the big deal about sin?" you may be thinking. "I am a good person. I help my neighbor with his groceries sometimes, and I hold the door for old ladies when going into the grocery store." Being good enough has nothing to do with sin. It goes much deeper than that.

The truth is that when we think about sin, we don't usually think about death. But God says that the penalty for sin is death: "The wages of sin is death" (Romans 6:23). It is not disputed that everyone will eventually grow old and die—that is the one thing we all have in common. So if we are all going to die anyhow, what is this talk about sin bringing death? What we often don't think about, however, is another type of death—spiritual death.

When Adam and Eve were placed in the garden of Eden, they were told to enjoy all of their surroundings and eat from all the trees there, but there was one tree in the middle of the garden they were not to eat from. God said the moment they ate from it they would die. Eventually the enemy tempted them to eat from the tree God told them not to eat from, and in the moment they took a bite of the fruit, they died. Of course it took them many years to physically die—they would go on to live for a long time after that. But in the very moment they ate from the tree God told them not to eat from, they died a spiritual death. They were separated from God because they had disobeyed Him.

Spiritual death forever separates us from God. If we die in our sin, then we will be separated from God for all eternity. The truth is that sin is not just a mistake. Rather, it is missing God's mark of perfection; it is choosing your own will and way rather than the perfect plan of Almighty God. Sin is turning your back to God and living life apart from Him. When not dealt with, sin always ends in death—separation from God in this life, and eternal separation from God in the life to come.

But there is good news to be told here: Eternal life is a gift from God. Paul again reminds the Romans: "But the gift of God is eternal life through Jesus Christ our Lord" (Romans 6:23). We don't earn or pay for a gift; we simply accept it and receive it with joyful gratitude. This gift from God comes to us through His one and only Son, Jesus Christ.

Our horrendous sin problem has a perfect solution—the Son of God. God made a way for sinful humanity to be reconciled back into a relationship with Him. This journey starts with recognizing our need, as we have already mentioned, then admitting that we can't save ourselves from sin. Next, we need to acknowledge that we desperately need God's gift of eternal life. Once we recognize our need, then we can more clearly see our need to receive the gift God offers us with thanksgiving and without reservation. We cannot save ourselves from our own proclivity to sin—we need someone to redeem us, to pay the price for us, so that we can receive the free gift.

Because we live in a fallen and sinful world, our understanding of what love is *is* utterly jaded. Love is not what is portrayed through the media on a daily basis, nor does a spouse or loved one telling you they love you exemplify it. God showed us what true love is by sending His only Son to die for us upon the cross. Why would He do this? It was because God loves us and wants a relationship with us: "God demonstrates His own love for us, in that while we were yet sinners Christ died for us" (Romans 5:8).

When Jesus died on the cross, He paid the price for all sin, and when He became sin Himself on the cross, He paid our ransom and freed us from sin and death. He gave Himself for our salvation when we were still lost in our sin because He loves us more than we will ever comprehend. His love is unfathomable—that He would die for you and me while we were sinners is incredible. But He did this to reverse the effects of sin in our life, to reverse the effects of Adam and Eve's choice so long ago.

If you no longer want to experience the separation between God and yourself, then simply ask God to help you grasp the extent of His love. While we were yet His enemies, He loved us enough to die for us so that the penalty for our sins was paid in full. This might be hard to grasp and understand fully, but its truth will penetrate our hearts and minds as we receive God's gift of salvation and walk by faith in Him one day at a time.

Receiving this free gift from God is not hard to do. How do we receive it then? That's easy. We simply call out to God and ask Him to forgive us and save us: "Whoever will call on the name of the Lord will be saved" (Romans 10:13). It's as simple as saying, "Jesus, forgive me of my sins and come into my heart." We acknowledge our need for God, thereby surrendering to His lordship over our lives.

Calling out to the Lord from a sincere heart is just that—calling out to Him. This means we talk to Him as we would talk to a friend standing next to us—praying, acknowledging that He is God and we are not. It's simple and yet incredibly profound. We can choose to live our lives apart from God, not recognizing our need for Him; or we can surrender the rule of our own lives and accept His instead.

If we choose to call out to the Lord for help in the midst of our sinfulness, there is something amazing that takes place. Paul wrote,

"If you confess with your mouth Jesus as Lord, and believe in your heart that God raised Jesus from the dead, you shall be saved; for with the heart man believes, resulting in righteousness, and with the mouth he confesses, resulting in salvation" (Romans 10:9–10). Confessing our sins to Him and believing that He has been raised from the dead results in salvation—the freedom from our sins.

If you believe this is true, then you must act on your belief by confessing with your mouth that Jesus is Lord over all creation, including the Lord of your life. You are not your own any longer; you now belong to God. Belief starts in the heart and then moves you to action or confession, which results in salvation. Sin's grip no longer has a hold on you, and you now possess eternal life.

God loved you so much that He didn't leave you stuck in your sins, stuck in your eternal separation from Him. He provided a way out through the sacrifice of His Son upon the cross for your sins. If you have called out on the name of God today, then know that your relationship with Father God is restored. I would encourage you to find a church to get involved in that teaches the Bible, for you can't live the Christian life alone. Talking to God and reading the Bible every day are also great ways to deepen your newfound relationship with Jesus Christ. If you chose to call out to Jesus today, then you have just made the most important decision of your life.

ABOUT THE AUTHORS

ERIN KELLY is the older daughter of Jim and Jill Kelly. She has always had a passion for writing, journaling, and sharing her faith. A sought-after speaker to young women, Erin has coauthored five books with her sister, Camryn. She attends Liberty University in Lynchburg, Virginia.

JILL KELLY is the wife of retired Buffalo Bills quarterback and Pro Football Hall of Famer Jim Kelly. She is a speaker and the author of several books, including the *New York Times* best-seller *Without a Word*. She and Jim live in Buffalo with their daughters.

ACKNOWLEDGEMENTS

To my mommy and best friend: Words certainly fall short. I'm so thankful that God has allowed us to partner together in writing *Kelly Tough*. Thank you for sticking by my side through it all. For encouraging me, laughing with me, crying with me. Your love for Jesus is contagious. I want to be more like you because every day you long to be more and more like Him. You're my best friend and I am in awe that God has chosen you to be my mom. I love you so much…*more*!

To Daddy: Thank you for teaching me what it means to be *Kelly Tough*. For taking your teeth out and making Mommy, Cam, and me laugh! Thank you for trusting God and not giving up. Your resilience to defeat motivates me. I love you so much, Daddy… more than a million footballs!

To Cam: I couldn't have asked for a more amazing little sister. Your spunk and love for life make me smile! I have learned so much from you, Cam. I am so proud to be your big sister. Thank you for putting up with Mommy and me through the busyness of writing *Kelly Tough*. I love you, Cambam!

To Grammie: Thank you for relentlessly praying for me. You are the wisest and most compassionate person I know. Thank you for every moment where you've just listened. When I look at you I see Jesus and want to be more like Him. His wisdom pours out of you. I am so thankful that God has given me you. I love you…*more*!

To Grandpa: I am so thankful for you. The weekly cards you send to me at Liberty University have been such a huge blessing. Thank you for always thinking about me and praying for me! I love you.

To the Waggoner Clan: Uncle Jack, Aunt Kim, Ben, Paige, and Bradley…thank you for being prayer warriors! You're amazing. I love you all so much!

To Uncle Danny: I hope that I will always be a sibling that is as loyal as you are to my dad. Words are not enough to express how thankful I am for all that you have done for my father. You're an incredible brother. We love you!

To Uncle Ray: Thank you for being there for weeks on end, helping take care of #12. You always brought laughter and joy into the room—something that we all needed! We miss having you in Buffalo! We love you!

To the Kelly family, my dad's amazing friends, and my friends (you know who you are): Wow! If only you all knew how much you mean to us. Thank you for everything! For the prayers, smiles, laughter, food, support, balloons, flowers, chocolate-covered strawberries, and more! God's amazing love has been displayed through you all in countless ways!

To Tricia Cavalier: First of all, you're amazing and I don't know how you do what you do. If there's one blessing that came out of all that my dad had to go through, it's that I got to spend more time with you. Words fall so short as I try to thank you for all that you have done for our family. You are family! We love you! Thank you for always being there for us.

To all the doctors and nurses: There are too many to name here, but we will never forget you. Dr. Westermeier, Dr. Loree, Dr. Sullivan, Dr. McLean, Dr. Costantino, Dr. Shah, Dr. Hertz, and all the nurses at Lenox Hill and ECMC…and to the people who prepped and cleaned my dad's room, the people who brought us food and chocolate milk shakes, the pastoral staff…we cannot possibly thank you all enough for all that you did to take care of my dad. We have witnessed God's goodness through you all. Thank you so much! May the Lord bless and keep you.

To the fans: You are incredible! The letters, the signs, the hashtags, the T-shirts, the bracelets, the puzzles, the prayers…. You are one of the reasons that my dad was motivated to be Kelly Tough. Thank you!

To Mrs. Barber: You have been my "Southern Mama" since I came to Liberty my freshman year. Thank you for earnestly praying for me. And thank you so much for all our coffee dates and bringing me to the airport every weekend so that I could be with my dad in New York City. I am so thankful for you and your family! Love you all! Go Flames!

To the Falwell family and my LU family: I am so blessed and thankful that God chose to have me attend Liberty. I would not have survived everything that our family went through without the constant prayer, support, love, and encouragement of my LU family. I will be forever grateful! You are my family, and LU will always be my home away from home.

To Jana: The Kelly girls love you! Thanks for putting up with us and being a constant encouragement. I'm so thankful I can talk "football" with you and you totally get it! Thank you for believing in this book and pushing hard for it on our behalf!

To Rick: This book would be nothing without you. Thank you for not giving up on us. For adjusting your schedule to make sure you had time—no matter what time of the day or night. Your determination and encouragement kept us going. I have learned so much about writing through working with you, and I am truly grateful.

To David Sluka: Thank you for all you have done to make *Kelly Tough* a reality! Your patience and constant encouragement and insight have helped us to create what's written on these pages. Glory to God!

To Carlton Garborg: Thank you for believing in the greater *Kelly Tough* story and for giving us the incredible privilege of sharing what God has done in the midst of our pain. We are honored and blessed to work with you and the BroadStreet Publishing team.

To Jesus: Thank You that in our weakness You are strong. Thank You for the struggle, because through it we have found and embraced more of You! I love You, Lord. And thank You for healing my daddy!